CANCEL
Your Own
GODDAM
SUBSCRIPTION

CANCEL *Your Own* GODDAM SUBSCRIPTION

Notes & Asides
from *National Review*

WILLIAM F. BUCKLEY JR.

BASIC
BOOKS

A Member of the Perseus Books Group
New York

Published by Basic Books
A Member of the Perseus Books Group

Books published by Basic Books are available at special discounts for
bulk purchases in the United States by corporations, institutions,
and other organizations. For more information, please contact the
Special Markets Department at the Perseus Books Group,
2300 Chestnut Street, Suite 200, Philadelphia, PA, 19103 or call (800) 255-1514,
or e-mail special.markets@perseusbooks.com.

Set in 11 point Minion by the Perseus Books Group

Library of Congress Cataloging-in-Publication Data
Buckley, William F., Jr. (William Frank), 1925–
    Cancel your own goddam subscription : notes & asides from National
Review / William F. Buckley, Jr.
        p.   cm.
    ISBN-13: 978-0-465-00242-9 (hardcover : alk. paper)
    ISBN-10: 0-465-00242-0 (hardcover : alk. paper) 1. Buckley, William F., Jr.
(William Frank), 1925– 2. National Review—History. 3. United States—Politics
and government—1945–1989. 4. Journalists—United States—Biography.
I. Title.
PN4874.B796A3 2007
841'.4—dc22   2007004715

10 9 8 7 6 5 4 3 2 1

For Linda Bridges

—Devotedly

CONTENTS

"HANGING" EARL WARREN, CONSORTING WITH GOD

October 1967–April 1972

*N*ATIONAL *REVIEW* MAGAZINE began publishing in November 1955. I was its founder and editor and only stockholder. We began with a very small subscription list, but it was made up of lively and expressive people. Most letters addressed to us for publication were satisfactorily dealt with by simply sending them to the magazine's letters section. Others cried out for different treatment. Gradually the thought crystallized that those who wrote to us exercising special skills or leaving a special flavor should not be treated perfunctorily.

I began to channel unorthodox letters into a department I called "Notes & Asides." That department evolved as my own personal page in the magazine, available for whatever purposes I had in mind to put it to. Some correspondents made their points in special, even distinctive language. Some were curious, some disparaging, some downright combative. Most of these letters were answered in print, or commented on in some way. Some of them led to exchanges that ran on to succeeding issues. Sometimes "Notes & Asides" was used to reproduce personal bulletins I thought of interest to at least some of our readers. These included occasional letters addressed by me to publishers or public figures.

The feature was popular, and its life was extended after my retirement. This came in two stages. In 1990 I retired as hands-on editor-in-chief; in 2004, I gave away my ownership of the magazine. But "Notes & Asides" survived, perhaps not quite as robust as in its prime, but with more than life enough to warrant the occasional column of space in which it spoke with its distinctive orientation.

At the suggestion of Ed Capano, our publisher from 1991 until his retirement in June 2006, I agreed to bring together in book form material chosen from that huge body of work.

The intention here is to instruct and to divert. I don't doubt that this book will perform those services for regular readers of the magazine, but I suspect it will do so also—perhaps especially—for others who have never read *National Review*, but who are curious about life, and how the quiddities of life are sometimes expressed.

Much thought was given to how to present the material here. The initial idea was to organize it thematically. Letters were grouped under separate headings. I went to some pains to taxonomize forty years of work, with the critical help of *NR* Associate Editor Alston Ramsay, an agile editorial intelligence freshly with us after serving as editor-in-chief of *The Dartmouth Review*.

Finally, I judged that the thematic version didn't work. However, Mr. Ramsay could not take sufficient time away from the magazine to help produce a new version. It was great luck for us that another junior editor of *National Review* was friends with a graduate student (in comparative literature) from the University of Virginia, bound for Cambridge but with a month or two uncompromised. Charles Nicholas Chapin was guided by Occam's razor, the theory that the simplest approach is often the best approach. The result is here before you.

The material is presented chronologically—as it appeared in the magazine over four decades. The reorganization I found refreshing. There are no historical ambiguities. Impulsive thoughts and words are displayed pell-mell as if still hot from the muzzle that fired them. And moving through the harum-scarum of comments livid and tender, lively and pedantic, we are directly in touch with the journalistic incubator that brought it all forth.

What we then did was divide the material into four sections. The first, beginning in the turbulent late 1960s, runs roughly (to use Roman historical friezes) from Johnson II through Nixon I, never mind that Mr. Johnson and Mr. Nixon hardly show their faces in these fifty pages—they serve as bookends. Section 2 takes us through Watergate and the Carter malaise. Section 3 ushers in the Reagan years. Finally, in Section 4, we go through the last throes of the cold war and some of the attendant tensions, to the challenges of the next decade.

The mail brought every now and then a true surprise. I like to recall one letter, claiming to come from a high-school student, so stunningly precocious I thought it phony. But I published Edward Vazquez and got to know him when he matriculated at Columbia. We were in regular touch during his college years. ("Every time I turn around I'm being offered a scholarship. They think because my name is Vazquez I am an indigent Latino.") He came once or twice to the offices of *NR*, and wrote two book reviews for us. On graduating he sought employment in the State Department, and for whatever it might be worth to him, I gave him a To Whom It May Concern recommendation which would have been just right for John Adams. I know that he was accepted, and am sorry not to have had word from him since then, thirty-five years ago.

The reader will also find in the first section tastes of the tough language of the day (should we hang Earl Warren?), a counter-roast of black essayist and novelist James Baldwin, a young student—the same Vazquez—who wants to know what exactly is meant by immanentizing the eschaton. Senator Edward Kennedy calls attention to his fiscal husbandry, and wishes me speedy passage to the DMZ in Vietnam. The pulsations of the period are expressively reacted to by individual correspondents.

And President Nixon, having returned from China, where his every step was watched by "us"—the eighty-three journalists who accompanied him—writes to accept my resignation from the outer fringes of his administration: "It was with regret that I learned of your decision . . . " The letter was written three months before the Watergate break-in, and much regretting lay ahead.

∽

October 17, 1967

Channel 13
N.Y.C., N.Y.

Dear Sir:

It has bothered me sufficient times to warrant my taking pen in hand to ask for your assistance. Mr. Buckley seems to be listing to the left (a side on which he feels most uncomfortable) all the time. To me it has a disturbing value, for I keep questioning--"Is the chair broken? Can it be so every week?"

Perhaps he has concluded this peculiar position allows for a unique camera angle and gives him an advantage.

"Is it possible," I ask myself, "he has a problem with his back?"

Maybe he never sat up straight at Yale or even before that!

Hasn't any other viewer noticed it? Or am I seeing his position incorrectly?

Respectfully,
Mack Rapp, Senior Consultant
Rapp & Rapp & Associates Inc.
Port Washington, N.Y.

Dear Mr. Rapp: Channel 13 forwarded your kind letter in which you express concern for my back. I suffer no pains, so I have no excuse other than my natural slouchiness. Might I make a suggestion? Why don't you tilt over when you watch the program until the long axis of your body and that of mine are exactly parallel? Try that and I think you will find that the only thing that then distracts you is my main guest, who will appear to be at an angle. But since each guest adopts a slightly different posture, there will unquestionably be an agreeable variety to compensate for this. Yours cordially, WFB

October 31, 1967

Mr. Buckley:

  You are the mouthpiece of that evil rabble that depends on fraud, perjury, dirty tricks, anything at all that suits their purposes.
  I would trust a snake before I would trust you or anybody you support.

A. Ruesthe
[no address]

Dear Mr. Ruesthe: What would you do if I supported the snake? Cordially, WFB

November 14, 1967

Dear Mr. Buckley:

  Is *National Review* ever going to do anything about the greatest piece of scum in American journalism? He dumps on everyone who loves America.

Sincerely,
Betty Patterson
Whittier, Calif.

Dear Mrs. Patterson: When we received your letter we were just about to act. See below. Cordially, WFB

Announcing
A New Patriotic Committee
JOIN NOW

THE NATIONAL COMMITTEE
TO HORSEWHIP
DREW PEARSON

—Whereas by his foul insinuations on the virtue of Mrs. Shirley Temple Black, Mr. Drew Pearson has outraged the conscience of the community;

THEREFORE: We do hereby propose, and solicit support for, The Committee to Horsewhip Drew Pearson.

Honorary Sponsors: **Harry Truman, Esq.**
Dwight D. Eisenhower, Esq.
Majority Whip, U.S. Senate
Minority Whip, U.S. House of Representatives

Partial List of Honorary Members
(appointed without prior consultation)

Adolph A. Berle	Hon. Kenneth B. Keating	Hon. Ronald Reagan
Hon. Thomas E. Dewey	Hon. Francis Knight	Hon. Mendel Rivers
Hon. Thomas J. Dodd	Hon. Henry Cabot Lodge	Francis Cardinal Spellman
Hon. Barry Goldwater	Hon. John W. McCormack	William A. White, Esq.
Hon. J. Edgar Hoover	Hon. William Miller	Walter Winchell, Esq.
Hon. Lyndon Baines Johnson	Hon. Richard M. Nixon	Lloyd Wright, Esq.

November 28, 1967

First, a report on the newest patriotic committee, the National Committee to Horsewhip Drew Pearson, launched by a few patriots as the only appropriate response to Mr. Pearson's slurs on Shirley Temple, and his willingness to sacrifice the future of two families in order to make a cheap sensationalist point involving Ronald Reagan. Well, the Committee is off to a flying start. Membership badges and buttons are offered at $2.00. (Write to "Horsewhip Drew Pearson," 150 E. 35th St., New York 10016.) As I write, the button is being forged in the factory, and early next week will be mailed out to what is likely to become the largest nonpartisan committee in the United States. Typical responses are "Delighted to join!" (Mr. E.V.C., Mechanicsburg, Ohio) "Thanks so much for this new and sorely needed committee. You've made it *fun* to be patriotic again!" (Mrs. M.R.H., San Diego, California) Mrs. T.S.L. from Clearwater, Florida sends $10 "for my membership and perhaps some needy students." Needy students, no Californians considered, please apply. Address: Scholarship Dept., Committee to Horsewhip Drew Pearson, address above. We shall keep you posted, and meanwhile, don't forget to wear your buttons at all public gatherings. A committee of Quakers visited us yesterday petitioning us to produce a second, luminous button, so as to keep the Committee's goal visible at all times. The Executive will consider the economic feasibility and report back in due course. —WFB

December 12, 1967

It appears that everybody in the entire world desires to become associated with the National Committee to Horsewhip Drew Pearson, with the result that the Board of Directors has decided to limit charter membership to 10 per cent of the population of the United States. So that if you desire to join, write to Horsewhip Drew Pearson, 150 E. 35th St., New York 10016; or wire or cable, HORSEWHIP CARE NAT WEEKLY NEW YORK. First come, first served. The buttons now exist, and will be mailed out, along with membership certificates, towards the end of this week. The NCHDP Executive Whip, C. H. Simonds, has announced that the Committee will also supply little round stickers, appropriate for affixing to loci of moral indignation. They should regularly decorate your letters to your congressmen. They are available at $1.00 for 25, minimum order $1.00.

You will recall that a lady philanthropist sent in an extra eight dollars designated for scholarship memberships for needy students, from whom we have heard in droves. Mr. R. H. Jr. of Glen Ellyn, Illinois, who petitions for a scholarship, writes: "I am a needy student just barely getting through the seminary and feel thwarted in my deep passionate desire to horsewhip the Infidel." (R. H. Jr. won one of the scholarships.) Another comes in from Mr. F. T. of Troy, New York: "Last year my resources were worn so thin that I took to eating rice and beans fourteen meals a week, and nothing the other seven meals. And last month, when I was down to my last $30, I spent $6.89 on a *National Review* subscription. Furthermore, I feel that Drew Pearson needs to be horsewhipped. Who can be needier?" Not very many people can be needier, Brother F.: and in recognition that man cannot live by bread alone, we offer you membership, gratis, in Horsewhip. Mr. Dick Sartwell, President of the Associated Students of Malone College in Canton, Ohio, wants to know: "Is there anything wrong with starting a campus committee for said purposes?" Certainly not, the Executive Whip advises, suggesting a riding crop as the appropriate symbol for junior membership. And Michael D. Hoffman of Wilmette, Ill., wishes to donate his services to form a "Young NCHDP—after all, shouldn't youth be protected from Drew Pearson too?" Young Mr. Hoffman has received his franchise.

What, meanwhile, has the whippee to say about all this? One of the Committee recently heard him interviewed on the air. What did he think about the Committee to Horsewhip Drew Pearson? "Well," Mr. Pearson answered, "the man behind it all was for Joe McCarthy ten years ago, what else can you expect?" "And besides," Mr. Pearson added, "the Committee is asking two dollars for a membership, whereas I would like people to send me *four* dollars, which *I* would send on to the Boys Club of America." We checked with the President of the Boys Club of America, who observed: "Flattery will get Mr. Pearson nowhere. The Boys Clubs are organizing Horsewhip Drew Pearson Committees all over America. If he thinks he can bribe us, he underestimates the moral fiber of American youth."

So don't forget, the Committee has only a couple of weeks left to accept membership. Act fast. —WFB

December 26, 1967

And a bulletin from the National Committee to Horsewhip Drew Pearson, from the Executive Whip: "Everything is in the mail. However, some of you have unclear handwriting, or else you wrote in such haste to inscribe yourselves as charter members of the Horsewhip Committee that your fingers trembled. In case your name appears wrong, please send in your certificate, and we'll give you another one, free, gratis."

You will find, when you begin wearing your buttons, proudly, that lots of people will approach you and, almost invariably, ask: "Why do you want to horsewhip Drew Pearson?"

To which there is one and only one answer authorized unanimously by the Committee, to wit, "Because of what he said about Shirley Temple."

Now don't go and gild the lily. That's ALL you should reply. Then tilt your head up just the least little bit, heavenward, and permit, perhaps, a tear to make its way slowly down your idealistic cheek, chick.

A very Merry Christmas to you, from your grateful friend and admirer, —WFB

January 30, 1968

Shall I reply to the lady from *Good Housekeeping*, who took it all so nicely? She had written in connection with a survey, to ask what my wife found most endearing in me, that might account for the success of our marriage ("We have had interesting replies from President and Mrs. Lyndon Johnson . . . "). I sent the note to my wife, who scrawled in pencil on the letter: "I have always had a passion for men with six toes. When I saw Mr. Buckley in his bathing trunks I noticed he had six toes in one foot, and eight in the other. Bliss! As soon as I saw his feet I asked for his hand, and we have been happily married ever since." The lady editor took it all in very good humor: "I knew it must have been hard to fill Mr. Buckley's shoes, and that there was more of him than meets the eye . . . " Whereupon C. H. Simonds, our valued associate, informed us that his half-brothers were born with six toes and six fingers; but that in an early operation they were cut down to size. Mr. Rickenbacker observed that that was a pity, since six fingers would be especially useful for pointing the fingers of scorn. The chairman brought the meeting to order.

Mr. Rickenbacker, by the way, sends up an uncompleted editorial paragraph, with the notation: "WFB: Could you finish this? I think I'm in over my depth." Perhaps *you* would care to finish it? It goes: "Suffering from an acute case of infarcted bloviasis of the fantod? Snew Hums, the only riggly chuff! Warsher over flintion! Driputed lexanalysis completely refirms the findings of the National Institution of Fantodiasis that regular daily soncumation of Hums, the riggly chuff, underarches the . . . " You have to understand Rickenbacker . . . —WFB

June 4, 1968

National Review
150 East 35th Street
New York, N.Y. 10016

Dear Sir:

I have before me several copies of printed matter issued by your organization. I feel that you are friendly to organized labor, but note the omission of the New York Allied Printing Trades Council Union Label on the printing referred to.

The more than 2,000,000 members of labor unions in Greater New York, together with their friends, look for the Allied Union Label on printing. It is the only emblem recognized by the general labor movement as an assurance that the literature was produced under fair conditions in this city.

I feel that you will appreciate having your attention called to this matter.

May we anticipate that you will give consideration to this matter in the same friendly spirit in which it is presented, and that you will advise us of your cooperation to our mutual benefit.

Very truly yours,
Theodore A. Quets
Director, Label Department
New York Typographical Union No. 6
62 West 14th Street, N.Y.
Bertram A. Powers, President

Dear Mr. Quets:

When you grant your typographers the right to work without joining your organization, I will believe that you speak for them. Until then, I would no more attach your label to a freeman's magazine, than I would display the emblem of a work-camp. Moreover, National Review *would not want its public to think that it was in any way associated with an organization whose consideration for the public is measured by its willingness, during the past few years, to deprive it of all newspapers for a period of five months, and, finally, to force four newspapers into extinction. Perhaps you will, as Director, Label Department, communicate to other publications their option of putting a small "NR" on the corner of an inside page, to signify that a Brotherhood survives which hopes one day to be liberated from your monopolistic yoke. I thought you would appreciate having your attention called to this alternative.*

Yours faithfully,
Wm. F. Buckley Jr.

July 2, 1968

We note that Mr. William F. Alexander, the assistant district attorney in Dallas who helped prosecute Jack Ruby, has been allowed to resign for having remarked a few weeks ago that "Earl Warren shouldn't be impeached, he should be hanged." As the source of this rather infamous jest—it appeared originally (Sept. 29, 1961) in these pages, in the introduction to an article on the question whether Earl Warren should be impeached (no)—we can well understand Mr. Alexander's superior, Mr. Henry Wade, declaring that "that was not a very nice thing to say." No indeed: which is why we said it, niceness being beside the point we originally sought to convey, namely that there were, and are, no constitutional grounds on which to impeach Earl Warren, undesirable though he is as Chief Justice.

The night John Kennedy was shot, we found ourselves staring, incredulous, at Huntley and Brinkley, one of them saying to the other, what could you expect but violence in a country in which a prominent national magazine "comes out for" hanging Earl Warren? "Of course," said David to Chet or Chet to David, "they pretended they said it in jest. . . . but . . . " But? In what way did Mr. Alexander say it? Unless he said it in jest, he shouldn't have been fired, he should have been hanged. Did Stephen Decatur really mean to damn the torpedoes to eternal perdition? What did the torpedoes ever do to him? Ah, my lords, and oh, my lieges, what a dreadful time we are going to have maintaining the robustness of the English language. It is only obscenity that you can get away with these days. If Mr. Alexander had alleged that Mr. Warren had incestuous relations with his mother, no one would have noticed him, except maybe Norman Mailer and other flypapers of licentious tang. Hang it all. (Okay.) Hang 'em all. (No. Huntley-Brinkley no like.) —WFB

August 13, 1968

I have been sent a tearsheet from *West Magazine* (published by the *L.A. Times*), an excerpt from an interview with James Baldwin. I pass along one paragraph: "Then there were the fabled debates with William Buckley, one at Oxford which Baldwin won hands down, with the first standing ovation accorded anyone in this century; one in New York which he lost because 'I was trying to do what Martin was doing, I still hoped one could make people listen. But Bill's a bully, he can't listen, he uses weapons I simply won't use. I said people who live in the ghetto don't own it, it's white people's property. I know who owns Harlem. He said, "Do the landlords tippy-toe uptown and throw the garbage out the windows?" And I tuned out. If a cat said that to me in life, I'd simply beat the hell out of him. He was saying Negroes deserved their fate, they stink. To my eternal dishonor, I cooled it, I drew back and I lost the debate. I should have beat him over the head with the coffee cup. He's not a serious man. He's the intellectuals' James Bond.'"

1) It was Cambridge, not Oxford. 2) It was billed as a debate, but wasn't one, really. Mr. Baldwin delivered a set speech, uninterrupted by questions, sat down, and never raised his voice again. He received the standing ovation before I had uttered a single word. With my genius for ingratiation, I pointed out to the young English bloods that their reception of Mr. Baldwin, coupled with their demonstrated ignorance of his work either in fiction or as an essayist, neatly demonstrated their penchant to patronize Mr. Baldwin because he is i) Negro, ii) an intellectual, and iii) anti-American. I subsequently lost the popular vote by approximately 3–1; but I won a whole lot of other things. 3) It isn't clear just what are the weapons that Mr. Baldwin is not prepared to use. For instance, he has written that the only thing that white people have that Negroes should want is power. He finds America racked by hatred, empty of generosity, mad with sexual envy, besotted by Christian superstition. Christ was a "sunbaked Hebrew fanatic." I cannot think of any "weapons" of a complementary sort that I have ever even considered using against the Negro race or Negro culture. 4) Mr. Baldwin is visibly unhappy with the logical limitations of his own analysis. The throwing of garbage outside one's window or into one's own backyard is a sign of demoralization and/or sloppiness altogether extraracial (Peter Stuyvesant complained in the seventeenth century about the

practice in Manhattan). Mr. Baldwin's resentment at attention being drawn to the limitations of his social analysis is an index rather of his paranoia, than of other people's sadistic racism. 5) It is not necessarily a pity that he should have experienced the temptation to physical violence, but it is a pity that he should now regret that he suppressed that temptation, thus associating himself with that regrettable class of people in the South who are quoted, mostly in fiction to be sure, as believing that the way to argue with dissidents is to "beat the brains out of that uppity nigger." No doubt Mr. Baldwin, who is disposed to use coffee cups to drive home his points, could learn how best to use them by carefully studying the reflexes of James Bond. —WFB

December 3, 1968

Dear Mr. Buckley:

  You ridiculous ass.

  If you really enjoy screaming about so-called leftwingers in academia, you have a long job ahead of you. Part of the reason there are so many of them is that anyone with any brains is what you people label "leftwingers." Fortunately the people who run universities ignore you. At Wayne State University there is an Assistant Professor of Philosophy named Richard Sharvy who is permitted to teach classes filled with young impressionable minds even though he is under a federal indictment for draft refusal.

  That's because nobody who matters pays any attention to clowns like you.

Sincerely,
Richard Sharvy
Detroit, Mich.

Dear Mr. Sharvy: Ho ho ho! Nobody who matters pays any attention to us,
eh? Ho ho ho. See you in the Mekong Delta, Sharvy. —WFB
(Copy: Tricky Dick)

Dear Mr. Buckley,

  My name is Tish Willis and I am a 14-year-old girl.
Many people think I am weird because I like you. I don't
think so. I am perhaps your greatest fan! I read your
column (in the *News American*) every time it's in there.
My social studies teacher who is pro-Humphrey asked us
who we thought would be president in 1972. I said "If
Nixon chooses not to run (notice how I throw these
clever ones in?), then I think Ronald Reagan will run
and win." Then my teacher said, "Who would you like to
see in the White House, out of anybody?" There were the
typical answers such as McCarthy, Lindsay and then I
said, "William Buckley." Half of the class said "Who's
he?" (They're so dumb!) And the other half laughed. So
did my teacher. I hope you won't throw this letter out
because I'm just a 14-year-old girl, but, after all,
in 7 years I'll be a voter and I will be voting the
Republican conservative ticket (and there's not many
of us left!). I would like to ask you a question, Mr.
Buckley, if you don't mind. Do you think we should lower
the voting age? I am against it. I think it should be
raised to 25. If I seem a bit garrulous, I will stop
writing, but could you please, maybe, write back?

Love,
Tish Willis
Baltimore, Md.

Dear Tish: I think you should be allowed to vote, but not the other girls in
your class, and certainly not your teacher. Love, WFB

Dear Mr. Buckley:

  Congratulations! Never have I subscribed to a
magazine and had it arrive so promptly. Thanks for
a great service.

Nancy Rice
Houston, Texas

Dear Miss Rice: It must have been an accident. You just can't trust those machines. Regards, WFB

January 6, 1969

Inasmuch as I am encouraged by my colleagues to fill this space as I please, I take liberties. Or do I? What follows is primarily of interest to syntacticians. How many of them are there? Not many. But—ah!—how many voyeurs? What follows is interesting, also, to students of friendship, nothing less than an assiduous case of which could have prompted the redoubtable Professor Hugh Kenner to such heroic efforts to demonstrate the demerits of a single English sentence. . . .

HK to WFB September 19, 1968

. . . Garry [Wills] under pressure tends to deliquescent metaphor (vide his Miami piece, *NR*), as does WFB to filigree syntax (vide current *Esquire*, first sentence, which while it parses [to say which is to say that a chicken coop does not collapse] resembles less a tensioned intricacy in the mode of M. Eiffel than it does a toddler's first efforts with Tinkertoy).

WFB to HK October 1

. . . You are surely wrong about that lead sentence? I re-read it, found it springy and tight.

HK to WFB October 15

. . . about that *Esquire* lead: it reads in my copy: "*Robert F. Kennedy had a way of saying things loosely, and it may be that that is among the reasons why so many people invested so much idealism in him, it being in the idealistic (as distinguished from the analytical) mode to make large and goodsounding generalities, like the generality he spoke on April 5 after the assassination of Martin Luther King, two months exactly before his own assassination.*"

"Springy and tight" my foot. Those aren't springs, they're bits of Scotch tape. Have your syntactic DNA checked for mutations; it just isn't governing the wild forces of growth as of yore.

WFB to HK October 17

Come on now, you are a goddam professor of English, so stop namecalling and get to work. . . .

HK to WFB October 25

. . . Okay, that sentence: One way of putting the problem is that it's not discernibly heading anywhere; it ambles along, stuffing more and more odds & ends into its elastic bag, until it simply decides to sit down. Mr. Niemeyer has ridiculed my interest in syntactic energy, countering my regret that Johann Sebastian Bach should be taking out the garbage with his pleasure that it's being taken out, whazzamatter, don't I want a tidy house? Yet I revert to the concept: something, something corresponding to tension and relaxation, to the turn of the key and the swing of the door, to departure from and return to the tonic, makes us willing to accept the necessity of a long sentence being one sentence and not three spliced by mispunctuation. Back to the exhibit: if there were a period after "loosely" no one would feel that a flight had been arrested in mid-course. Or after "him," or after "generalities." I think one test of the long sentence is that if it's stopped before it's over the reader should sense the incompleteness. This is sometimes a matter of formal grammar: if we start with "because" the reader won't accept a full stop until he's been accorded a principal clause. It's sometimes just a matter of promising in the opening words or by the opening cadence (a device of Gibbon's) some amplitude of concern the reader expects to see implemented. But here the offer to develop the proposition that RFK had a way of saying things loosely creates no syntactic expectation because it's capable of standing as a sentence by itself; nor does it retrospectively command the rest of the sentence, because the sentence has managed to end not with an amplification of RFK's looseness but with a triplicated irrelevancy about the date.

"Robert F. Kennedy had a way of saying things loosely: large and good-sounding generalities which being in the idealistic (as distinguished from the analytical) mode help explain why so many people invested so much idealism in him: generalities like the one Martin Luther King's assassination prompted him to utter on April 5, just two months, as it happened, before he was assassinated himself."

A possible improvement, if one must include all those components. The main difference is that by putting the colon after "loosely" one gives notice that the opening clause will preside over the remainder, not simply join to the next section of track. Then repeat of "generalities" to hitch the peroration to the second member. And rearrangement of terminal items keeps the mention of King and *l'affaire Sirhan* from sounding like doodles irrelevantly prompted by "April 5." I do not offer the improved version as anything but an exercise; I wasn't writing the article and haven't in my blood the points you anticipated making, so all I can manage is a piece of engineering.

I do not fuss about your occasional sentences to preserve a professorial edge. I merely call attention to dangers when I chance to see them. You revise carefully, I know, and it never hurts to have a few explicit criteria of revision. One is the rationale of the long sentence, as above (and failing that rationale, or failing time to adequate one's drafts to the rationale, vita being brevis and deadlines being yesterday, one ought, I think, to cut spaghetti into shorter sentences where natural stopping places occur). Another is that grammatical lint is best picked: in my suggested version I've avoided "that that," "reasons why" (your ear had told you to eschew yet a third "that"), and "it being." These all have rhetorical uses, as colloquialisms bounced off girders, but strung along in a row like old peanut shells they suggest WFB just plain improvising while he awaits a glimpse of daylight, and suggest to *les Dwight Macdonalds* that the Scrambled Egghead* method is to talk till one figures out what one is saying. This method is of course frequently necessary, and inoffensive, viva voce, say on TV, but its appearance should be avoided in print.

WFB to HK November 4

. . . I worry about that confounded sentence, as one worries upon failing to appreciate something which one is prepared to postulate as good, to wit your criticism of it. I shan't even apologize for belaboring the point, because I know that you will know that by talking back, I am proving that I have not put you to such inconvenience merely for my own amusement.

"Robert F. Kennedy had a way of saying things loosely" *followed by the colon you suggest means to me that I am about to demonstrate my allegation, or give an example of it. Followed by a period, the lilt of the sentence is, it seems to me, self-consciously dramatic, as in* "John F. Kennedy had a way of seducing women." *Followed by a comma, I thought it to be leading rather gradually to a point I did not want for a while yet, until the mood set in, to crystallize: whence, "*, and it may be that that is among the reasons why so many people invested so much idealism in him"—*again, if the period had come here, I'd have attempted, or so it strikes me, a stolen base, and the reader*

---

*Back in 1956 Macdonald had written for *Commentary* an attack on the fledgling *National Review* titled "Scrambled Eggheads on the Right."

would have been annoyed by the intimation that I have proved my point; or that I infer that the reader will merely permit me to asseverate it. Whence, i.e., by way of further explanation, begging the reader's indulgence so to speak, ", it being in the idealistic (as distinguished from the analytical) mode to make large and good-sounding generalities"—*department of amplification, but without—yet—the example I am about to furnish, and spend several hundred words confuting, ",* like the generality he spoke on April 5, after the assassination of Martin Luther King." *Surely writing about what Kennedy said about another man's assassination a few days after Kennedy's own assassination (which is when I wrote this article) gives a certain spooky suspense, which is ratified, Robert-Louis-Stevenson-wise, with the adverbial clause ",* two months exactly before his own assassination." *That last I take to be a fair substitute for* "two months exactly, as it happened, before his own assassination." *Seems to me that, although the sentence is long it is not impossibly long, and that although the commas appear somehow to be loose and thoughtless linkages they are justified by their meiotic contribution to the plot I am contriving. Hell, it merely disturbs me that while I understand your generic points, my ear does not grant them a pre-emptive relevance in this instance; and I repeat that I worry because undoubtedly you are right and I wrong. Anyway, I shall remember the generic advice. Believe. Me. Pal.*

HK to WFB November 7

. . . Not to wrangle, I'd make a final suggestion: that your inability to relate my comments, which you follow, to the sentence, the intentions of which you expound convincingly, is perhaps based on this, that you're not reading the printed sentence but hearing yourself speak it. By pause, by suspension, by inflection, by variation of tone and pace, you could make the "little plot" you speak of sing. The written language provides no notation for such controls, and your intention as graphed by printed words leaves the reader too much to supply, and too many options for supplying the wrong tacit commentary, e.g. that WFB is standing in an open space scattering peanut shells. We have no such public style as Pope could posit, and vary from minutely, in an aesthetic of microscopic inappropriatenesses. We have instead the convention that the writer creates his operating conventions de novo. "Robert F. Kennedy had a way of saying things loosely."—followed by a hypothetical period, you say, its lilt is self-consciously dramatic. Yes, but those are the very first words of a long essay; we are just tuning in to Station WFB; his eschewal of the self-consciously dramatic is not yet an operative principle; and one of the options open to us is to suppose that a dramatic opening was intended but muffed by a fault of punctuation. I think your rebuttal to my statement that the sentence could be terminated by a period at several points without creating a sense of incompleteness consists in an appeal to nuances of taste: it would make nuanced differences to cut it off here or here. So it would. But the reader hasn't yet a feel for the governing structure of taste in the piece before him. Especially in an opening, the reader would be well served by a syntactic tension, as inevitable as gravitation on an inclined plane, which makes it essential that the sentence incorporate, as it proceeds, the members it does, or else fall down. . . . Mais passons.

WFB urbi et orbe, Jan. 1, 1969: Who's right?

February 11, 1969

Dear Mr. Buckley:

   I am a sixteen-year-old High School Junior who is going, slowly but inexorably, out of his mind. I have come to the conclusion that you are the only person on the face of the earth who can save my sanity. My problem, briefly, is this: for the past year I have been trying, without avail, to discover just what, in God's name, the phrase "to immanentize the eschaton" means.

I heard you speak the phrase once on *Firing Line* and immediately made a valiant attempt to look it up. Upon discovering that my dictionary did not list the words I instantly resolved to ask one of my teachers in the morning.

When I tried this course I drew another blank. I would ask a teacher the question, whereupon he would have me repeat it a dozen or so times and then plead ignorance. I would then be asked: "Where'd you hear it?" When I informed him that you had used it the night before he would generally give me a forlorn look, mumble something like, "Oh him eh?," and express his innermost conviction, i.e., that you had probably invented the words. I'm sure you'll be thrilled to know, Mr. Buckley, that I had faith in you. I knew you hadn't invented those words. And, sure enough, when I was reading your book *The Unmaking of a Mayor* I came across a passage which revealed a Mr. Eric Voegelin as the author of the phrase. Jubilant, I raced to our school library and asked the librarian for everything written by Mr. Voegelin. "Never heard of him," the woman answered. As I left, ruminating upon the intrinsic failings of the public schools, I encountered the teacher to whom I had put the original question. When I explained the matter to him he expressed the conviction that, not only did you make up the phrase, but you also contrived Mr. Voegelin!

Now, Mr. Buckley, more than anything else in the world I would like to know what that phrase means. I really think you should tell me because: 1) I have watched every one of your TV shows and have read all of your newspaper columns ever since I first heard of you. And 2) I've read all of your books (save only the last one, *The Jeweler's Eye*, which, curse my parsimonious

soul, costs a small fortune. I'll wait 'til it comes
out in paperback). Also 3) I subscribe to *National
Review* and even read all of those silly renewal
notices I keep getting.

If all this evidence of my fidelity isn't enough then
I promise you that, if you somehow communicate to me
the definition, I will upon receipt of it: a) instantly
proceed to use it on any and all occasions and thereby
spread your fame far and wide (I make it generally
known to my friends that you are the source of my more
esoteric bits of verbiage) and b) I will renew my
subscription to *NR* the very next notice I get (which
will, no doubt, be Valentine's Day) instead of when
the thing expires as is logical.

Furthermore I shall c) badger my school librarian
until she finally breaks down and puts *NR* on the school
subscription list. After all, if the school can
subscribe to such egregious rags as *The Nation* and *The
New Republic* they can at least give your fine journal
equal time. Thanking you for your time in reading this
I remain

Sincerely yours,
Edward H. Vazquez
Old Bridge, N.J.

*Dear Edward: Eschaton means, roughly, the final things in the order of
time; immanentize means, roughly, to cause to inhere in time. So that to
immanentize the eschaton is to cause to inhere in the worldly experience and
subject to human dominion that which is beyond time and therefore
extraworldly. To attempt such a thing is to deny transcendence: to deny God;
to assume that Utopia is for this world. All of these things Professor Voegelin
draws out of the Gnostic heresy of yesteryear. His phrase, far from being a
contrivance of mine, is so famous that buttons actually exist, one of which I*

am sending you pinned into a copy of The Jeweler's Eye, *that bear the legend. "Don't let THEM immanentize the eschaton!" Tell your teachers they have a great deal to learn, not least the impeccable use of English, which you are manifestly equipped to teach them. Yours, WFB*

Dear Mr. Buckley,

   As a diversion from studying for a physics final, I was glancing through *The Jeweler's Eye* when I noticed, in the biographical section on the back of the dust jacket, that you have delivered, in round numbers, a total of one hundred million speeches. Assuming a total of fifty years of speaking, without weekends, holidays, or vacations, one would have exactly 18,250 days (this does not include leap years). Dividing 100,000,000 by 18,250, I calculate that you would have to make 5,475 speeches per day. Is the figure in the book a misprint, or perhaps the mischievous work of a typesetter at Putnam's?

Sincerely yours,
David L. Davies
San Bernardino, Calif.

Dear Mr. Davies: No, no mistake. That's about the right figure. Some of the speeches, of course, were short. Regards, WFB

August 26, 1969

Dear Mr. Buckley:

   In this writing--that I bring to your attention--I introduce myself to my readers saying: I am the Second Coming of Jesus of Nazareth. When I addressed a group at Times Square on August 6, proposing a new way to end war, I introduced myself to them also in the same way.

Now a person of your intelligence, your erudition, and refusal to accept surface appearance--your refusal to be mentally flim-flammed or deceived--your desire to search for the truth--should obtain great satisfaction in proving that an individual making such a claim is in fact an impostor--if that be the case.

Or--if despite the odds against it of billions to one-- if I am, in truth, who I say I am--and I repeat again: I am the second coming of Jesus of Nazareth--what more fantastic guest could you have on your program?

You stand to win—either way.

Norman Bloom
New York, N.Y.

Dear Mr. Bloom: Beware. I am the second coming of Pontius Pilate. —WFB

September 23, 1969

Dear Mr. Buckley:

Your syntax is horrible.

Ron Kelly
Mattoon, Ill.

Dear Mr. Kelly: If you had my syntax, you'd be rich. Cordially, WFB

October 7, 1969

Dear Mr. Buckley:

If my scrawl seems vaguely familiar to you, it's because I wrote to you about six or seven months ago, asking what an eschaton was and how one went about immanentizing it.

You were kind enough, not only to answer my question, but to publish my letter in the "Notes & Asides" section of *NR*.

Very happy at seeing something I'd written in print, I took great pains to carefully store the issue (Feb. 11, 1969) in which my bit of correspondence appeared. The Library of Congress, the New York Public Library, and the Smithsonian Institution having refused to preserve it under glass, I had to content myself with filing it in my desk. (Please bear with me, there really is a point to all this.)

The whole letter bit being done with, I proceeded to order my existence as usual. One of the things which I did was to write for applications and informational bulletins from several colleges which I am interested in attending. (Yale, Princeton, Harvard, Cornell, et al.)

The things they sent me were elucidating but disquieting, e.g., "President Kingman Brewster Jr., of Yale University, explaining the undergraduate admissions policy stated: 'For the class of 1973 there were 2,342,824.32057 applications for the 1,025 seats. Naturally, many worthy young people were rejected. Among those rejected were Jesus Christ and all twelve of his Disciples.' President Brewster explained that although Mr. Christ and his followers did meet Yale's minimum standards, they failed to impress the admissions committee with any 'special abilities or attributes, which though intangible, add immeasurably to any great university.' Besides, Yale is known to seek a religious and ethnic diversity. The fact that all thirteen were Christians of Semitic ancestry obviously didn't help."

My guidance counselor and I read all of this
over and he then asked me if I'd ever done anything
interesting. (Such as: climbing Mt. Everest or
teaching comparative philology to adolescent
gibbons.) "Well," I said, "I once had a rather long
letter published in the editorial department of a
national magazine. Any good?" "By all means," he
replied. I happily darted home to unearth my copy of
National Review, when, to my horror, I discovered
it was missing. Now my guidance counselor most
emphatically told me that if one isn't diverse
(say, a Cherokee Indian or a five-year-old that writes
operas) one must be interesting. Which brings me to
the point (at last) of this whole letter (book?).

I.e., are there any extra copies of the Feb. 11,
1969, issue of *NR* lying around your office that I might
purchase? If there are I would be most happy to pay any
costs (postage, detective fees, etc.) incurred in
getting them to me.

Finally, if I do succeed in getting into one of those
schools I mentioned (which I would dearly love to do
despite my kidding about their admissions policies)
maybe I can infiltrate the SDS [Students for a
Democratic Society] for you, or something.

Sincerely,
Edward H. Vazquez
Old Bridge, N.J.

*Dear Edward: If you don't get into the college of your choice, then I say, let
them immanentize the goddam eschaton. —WFB*

October 21, 1969

Clay Felker
Editor, *New York Magazine*
New York, N.Y.

Dear Clay:

Ideology launches a thousand ships every day, I know; but in civilized places, at least the effort is made to look honest about it. In your issue of September 15, your editors list the books of the forthcoming season, with comments, and divide them into two categories. Worth While and Worth Little. Under Worth Little I see: *"Odyssey of a Friend: Whittaker Chambers's Letters to William F. Buckley Jr., 1954–1961"* (Putnam). What can one say? What one can say is not a goddam thing. Because the ideologized imposter who put the book in that category had not even seen the book, not a single review copy having been sent out (the existing edition is privately printed). I do believe we have here the locus classicus of book-burning, liberal style. Do you agree?

Yours faithfully,
Wm. F. Buckley Jr.

P.S. Mr. Felker's answer will be published just as soon as it comes in, but remember, the mails are very slow.

Copy of a letter to an NR *advertiser:*

Dear Sirs:

I'm the drunk in your ad who doesn't really appreciate good bourbon. Rather, I drink to get smashed. However, now that you're advertising in *National Review*, I'm getting smashed on Beam's Choice.

Charles G. Nelson (Cpl)
Saigon, Vietnam

To the Editor
National Review

Sirs:

  Mr. William F. Buckley Jr. in his column makes the
following offer: "If anyone can find me one vote by
Sen. Kennedy in favor of one measure designed to
reduce government spending, I will retire to the
DMZ." We would point to Senator Kennedy's vote against
the ABM as evidence of his concern with wasteful
government spending on war.
  Would you be kind enough to inform us when Mr.
Buckley is leaving for the DMZ so we may arrange an
appropriate farewell party?

Richard D. Parker
Michael A. Heifer
Douglas Melamed
Harvard Law Review
Cambridge, Mass.

Dear Bill:

  When I read the first of your two recent columns
which concerned me, I was struck by your calm reasoning
and eminent good sense. When I read the second, I was
struck by your offer to retire to the DMZ if you
could find one vote by me on a measure to reduce
government spending.
  So I'm writing, first, to thank you for the kindness of
the earlier column. And I want to tell you, secondly,
that I have indeed voted to reduce government spending.
On September 19, 1967, for instance, I voted in
favor of an amendment to reduce by $21 million the
Independent Offices Appropriations Bill for fiscal
year 1968.

Included in this amendment was a sum of $1,177,000 for
a new federal building for Springfield, Massachusetts.
Shortly after this vote, when I returned to Western
Massachusetts, I learned that there is a lesson to be
drawn from economy in government: When you are the
senior Senator from Massachusetts, and you want to cut
federal spending, don't start by voting against a post
office in Springfield.

So I did want to point out that you haven't given
me proper credit for keeping my eye on the federal
budget. And I can assure you that the DMZ is not such
a bad place since we reduced the bombing.

Best regards,
Ted
DMZ

Dear Ted: You may resume bombing when ready. Now you have a sufficient motivation. Best, B.

November 18, 1969

Dear Mr. Buckley:

How do you square your "goddams" with your
Catholicism? Are you really blaspheming (which I
tend to doubt), or is there some distinction between
"goddam" (*NR*) and "God damn" with which I'm not
familiar? If so, I'd be interested to know how one
makes this distinction in the spoken word; also,
to have your definition and understanding of "goddam,"
not in my dictionary.

Ann Jones
New York Hilton Hotel

Dear Miss Jones: No. I am not really blaspheming, or in any case, do not mean to be blaspheming, blaspheming being one of those things I am against. "Goddam" is nowadays a simple expletive, an intensifier. It is that by cultural usage. In the most cloistered convent in Catholic Spain, you will hear from the venerable lips of an aged nun, "Jesus Mary and Joseph, I forgot my umbrella!" "I would pray hard to his Maker to save his soule notwithstanding all his God-damnes," a writer is quoted by the Oxford English Dictionary *as saying in 1647, back when they were fighting religious wars. Three hundred years later, the* American Heritage Dictionary of the English Language *lists "God damn" and "goddam" as "a profane [i.e., a-religious] oath, once a strong one invoking God's curse, now a general exclamation . . . used as an intensive." —WFB*

Dear Bill:

   New York Magazine is planning a special year-end
issue with a selection of short contributions from
influential people, and I hope you will want to
participate.
   I am asking each person to write fifty to two hundred
words on the following question:
   "If you had the power, what is the one change you
would make immediately in New York City?"
   The deadline for your answer is November 24, and we
pay an honorarium of $50.

Sincerely,
Clay Felker
Editor

Dear Sirs: In answer to your recent query, if I had plenipotentiary power in New York City I would decree that Mr. Clay Felker should be required to answer his mail. Yours faithfully, WFB

December 2, 1969

Dear Mr. Buckley:

  Regarding your polemics on profanity [Nov. 18]
I am somewhat comforted to know that you "do not mean
to be blaspheming" when you employ the "expletive"
God-dam. Further comfort may be derived from Thayer's
Greek-English lexicon of the New Testament which
ascribes blasphemy to those who by contemptuous speech
intentionally come short of the reverence due to
God or sacred things. Here the comfort ends, giving
place to a godly concern. For the Word of God--which
I equate with the Scriptures of the Old and New
Testament--specifically commands: "Thou shalt not
take the name of the Lord thy God in vain" (Ex. 20:7).
In the Hebrew the words "in vain" mean "to no good
purpose," thus, "thou shalt not take [use] the name of
the Lord thy God to no good purpose," which leads me to
believe that unless you are willing to argue that your
calling upon God to damn an inanimate or animate
object is purposive and conscionable, you are guilty
of transgressing the law of God, which is no light
thing. As one who professes the faith of Roman
Catholicism, I would expect you to yield more readily
to the "thus saith the Lord" of Exodus 20:7 than to the
culturally conditioned value of the *American Heritage
Dictionary of the English Language*.

Sincerely,
(Rev.) George Miladin
Reformed Presbyterian Church
Woodland Hills, Calif.

Dear Dr. Miladin: The meaning of words is established by their usage, which would suggest that blasphemy is defined by that which is intended, rather than by that which is spoken, at least in such cases as permit of ambiguity. In such cases, one should invoke the transcendent virtue: Charity shall cover the multitude of sins. I Pet. 4:8. —WFB

December 30, 1969

Mr. Buckley:

In promulgating your esoteric coagitations or in articulating your superficial sentimentalities or psychological observations beware of platitudinous ponderosity. Please let your conversations on TV and your editorials in *NR* possess clarified consciseness, compacted comprehensiveness, coalescent consistency and cocatinated cogency. Eschew all conglomerations, goddams, blasphemous incantations, flatulent garrulity, jejune babblement and assinine affectations. Let your extemperaneous decantations and unpremeditated expatiations have intelligibility without rhodomontade or thrasmonical bombast. Sedulously avoid all polysyllabical profundity, pompous prolixity and ventriloqual verbosity. Shun double entendre and prurient jocosity, whether obscure or apparent--longorrheic or otherwise.

Earl J. Beck
[no address]

Me Bill. Me no like-um Beck. Bad Beck. —WFB

January 27, 1970

Lawrence K. Miller, Editor
The Berkshire Eagle
Eagle Publishing Company
Pittsfield, Mass.

Dear Mr. Miller:

   I should have thought that you put a high enough value on your readers to protect them against columns written by a "notorious antisemite." In the event that that isn't the case, you are less fastidious than I am. Because I would not want to be associated with any newspaper disposed to tolerate among its regular writers a notorious antisemite. Under the circumstances, a) you should fire me because you believe the characterization of me by [the columnist] George Connelly (your issue of Oct. 6, 1969) to be true; or b) you will disavow the charge and apologize for having printed the libel, and perhaps take the opportunity to say what is your policy towards columnists who pass their libels through your pages; or c) I shall—just to begin with—instruct my syndicate to withdraw my column effective immediately.

Yours faithfully,
Wm. F. Buckley Jr.

Dear Mr. Buckley:

   Thank you for your letter of October 13 addressed to Lawrence K. Miller. In response thereto the marked item enclosed was appended to the October 20 column of Professor George G. Connelly.

Yours obediently,
Robert B. Kimball
Assistant to the Editor

[Enclosure:]

"Apology. Prof. Connelly, in a column of Oct. 6 based in part on an article by Gore Vidal in the September issue of *Esquire*, imputed anti-semitism to William F. Buckley Jr. Upon examination of all available evidence . . . an apology is tendered Mr. Buckley on behalf of our columnist and this newspaper. —Ed."

Lawrence K. Miller, Editor
The Berkshire Eagle

Dear Mr. Miller:

I note that not only are you too busy to prevent your columnists from submitting libels, you are also too busy to take the time personally to apologize to the victim for publishing them. I note also that the normally verbose Mr. Connelly is suddenly struck dumb, leaving it to others to apologize to me on his behalf. I am not disposed to have dealings with such people: not even professional dealings. On the other hand I do not wish to satisfy myself at the expense of such of your readers as desire to read my column. Under the circumstances, I shall continue to send you my column on the regular basis, on the understanding that you will not henceforward pay any money for it. I shall myself absorb the cost of mailing. Perhaps you and Mr. Connelly can meet and giggle together at this demonstration that crime can, after all, pay.

Wm. F. Buckley Jr.

February 10, 1970

Arthur Schlesinger Jr., Esq.

Dear Arthur:

I hope that Mr. Steibel [the producer of *Firing Line*] inaccurately reported a conversation with you concerning a proposed appearance on

Firing Line. He told me that you declined to appear on the program because you do not want to "help" my program, and you do not want to increase my influence, although to be sure you hope that the program survives. It seems to me that the latter desire is by definition vitiated by the initial commitment. If all the liberals who have appeared on *Firing Line* reasoned similarly, it would necessarily follow that the program would cease to exist—or is it your position that other liberals should appear on the program, but that you should not? And I should have thought it would follow from your general convictions that a public exchange with me would diminish, rather than increase, my influence. And anyway, the general public aside, shouldn't you search out opportunities to expose yourself to my rhetoric and wit? How else will you fulfill your lifelong dream of emulating them?*

Yours cordially,
Wm. F. Buckley Jr.

March 10, 1970

Dear Mr. Buckley:

I couldn't suppress a smile upon recalling the day of our meeting. When I entered your offices I spoke to the switchboard operator to ascertain the location of your office. She then called Miss Bronson to verify my appointment. Upon learning that you were tied up on the telephone she asked me to sit down for a few minutes. When I did so she was completely obscured by

---

*Nine years earlier, in the course of a debate, Mr. Schlesinger said of me, moving in for the kill: "He has a facility for rhetoric which I envy, as well as a wit which I seek clumsily and vainly to emulate." I had joyously used that phrase as a blurb on my next book, *Rumbles Left and Right*, which did not amuse Mr. Schlesinger.

the switchboard upon which she was frantically taking
calls. Every five seconds or so she would say: "Mr.
Buckley will be with you in a moment." To which I would
dutifully reply with some inanity. It took me about ten
repetitions to finally realize: No, idiot, she's not
talking to you, but rather to the dozen or so people
trying to reach Mr. Buckley. Thank God she didn't hear
me or she surely would have thought me a psychiatric
case in which you had taken an interest.

I look forward to hearing from Yale and Princeton,
as they are the only colleges to which I've applied
that haven't interviewed me.

Sometimes these interviews can call for great
intestinal fortitude and courage. I recall having
gone to Columbia about a month ago only to be greeted
at the door of the admissions office by 25 or so black
militants who were in the process of seizing it.
One character was standing in the vestibule with a
bull-horn haranguing the assemblage about Columbia's
perfidy vis-à-vis black students. I overheard him say:
"The only reason Columbia has blacks is to win the
football games for them." I remarked that if that
were true then Columbia would be lily-white since
the football team hadn't been doing that well of late;
no one thought me particularly humorous. There then
followed a dissertation on the advisability of making
it physically unsafe for Caucasians to roam Columbia,
at which point I went inside for my interview. The
interviewer motioned me to my seat and asked me what
most impressed me about Columbia. "Its similarity to a
combat zone," I answered. He found my rejoinder
somewhat inscrutable and asked that I explain myself.
I replied that: "Well, within the past five minutes I
was just accused of being a white racist (which I most
assuredly am not) and had my life indirectly

threatened by about 25 black militants who are, by the
way, in the process of seizing your office."

"Don't you think that these demonstrations have an
educational value?" he asked me. I didn't know whether
to laugh or withdraw my application. Instead I said
to him:

"It's not the sort of education for which I'd pay
$5,000.00 a year. It's sort of like asking a passenger
on the *Titanic* to assess the educational value of his
ticket." I got the distinct impression that the
interviewer wasn't too fond of me.

My other interviews have, happily, been somewhat more
peaceful.

Sorry to be so long-winded but when I start it's hard
to stop. I'll write you again when I find out how this
whole thing comes out (probably around April 15).

Sincerely yours,
Ed Vazquez

March 24, 1970

Dear Bill:

I do not see *The National Enquirer* or *National Review*
or whatever it is called; but I understand that you ran
your silly letter of January 15 to me in your issue of
February 10. I gather also that in neither this nor the
succeeding issue did you run my reply of January 30,
though it had obviously been in your hands in plenty of
time. In a better world I might have hoped that you
would have had the elementary fairness, or guts, to
provide equal time; but, alas, wrong again.

Sincerely yours,
Arthur Schlesinger Jr.

Dear Arthur:

I should have thought you would be used to being wrong. But to business. . . . Now, suppose I had begun this letter, "Dear Arthur, or Dear Barfer, or whatever you call yourself"? Would I do that? No; and not merely because it's childish, but because it isn't funny. The reason I did not publish your reply to my original letter is that I thought it embarrassingly feeble and it did not come to me with your permission to publish it. But, of course, now that you have relieved me of responsibility, I shall proceed to release it [see below].

One night, two or three years ago, you leaned over to me during a television broadcast when Lyndon Johnson was speaking about conservation, and whispered, "Better redwoods than deadwoods." I granted you, on the strength of that, a plenary indulgence. But that crack must have worked hell on your batteries, and it is obviously going to take a few years before they are capable of another successful discharge. Meanwhile I beg you, visit not your wit on me. Manifestly, it hurts you more than it hurts me.

Yours faithfully,
Wm. F. Buckley Jr.

Mr. Schlesinger's unpublished reply to WFB's January 15 letter:

Dear Bill:

Can it be that you are getting a little tetchy in your declining years? Nothing would give me greater pleasure than debating you on neutral ground; you are quite right in detecting my feeling that such public exchanges would diminish rather than increase your influence. But is it really lèse-majesté to suggest that I am under no obligation to promote your program? As for others, let them make their own decision. Don't tell me that you have stopped believing in freedom of

individual choice! You remind me of my other favorite
correspondent, Noam Chomsky.

Best regards,
Arthur Schlesinger Jr.

May 19, 1970

Dear Bill:

It should have been obvious even to you, I would have
thought, that the reason one confuses *The National
Enquirer* and the *National Review* is because they have
comparable standards of wit, taste, intelligence and
reliability. I am interested to see you so sensitive
on this point.

As for your decision to excommunicate me (again), I
fear that this is a weightier matter from your viewpoint
than from mine. The notion that the withdrawal of your
approval must, of course, bring your adversaries
immediately to their knees could commend itself only
to an egomaniac. And, lest you are in doubt, you have my
permission to publish this letter too.

Sincerely yours,
Arthur Schlesinger Jr.

Dear Arthur:

It is obvious to me that only someone who had difficulty in
distinguishing between *The National Enquirer* and *National Review*
could have written such works of history as you have written.

Nor have I intended to suggest that I have driven you to your knees,
merely that you should spend more time on them before presuming to
challenge

Your patient nemesis,
Wm. F. (Envy His Rhetoric) Buckley Jr.

July 28, 1970

Sir:

I read your column in the [*New York*] *Post* of May 6 and
have clipped the same to place it among my memorabilia
of some of your paranoic writings.

This one hits the lowest rung. You are a hateful
un-Christian demagogue and a fit associate for
loudmouth Rusher* who on a television program which
I recorded gave liberalism a slight pat on the head.

This is a time for righteous anger. I don't know
whether the Lord should damn or save your little
frightened cringing soul. Have you no concern or pity?
Sometime say something nice.

Carl E. Jampel
New York, N.Y.

*Dear Mr. Jampel: I love sugar, I love tea. I love the girls, and the girls love
me. Best, WFB*

Dear Mr. Buckley:

Not infrequently when I read your column I am
convinced that one or the other of us must be stark,
staring mad. Naturally, since I am only human and you
are quite possibly not, I conclude that it is you who
are mad.

After reading your May 19 column I must ask you to
have yourself committed. One cannot contend that the
United States might "button up the situation" in
Cambodia after observing our ineptitudes in Southeast

---

*William A. Rusher, the publisher of *National Review*, was one of the principals on
the television debate show *The Advocates*.

Asia and at the same time lay claim to one shred
of sanity.

It would serve no purpose for me to set out my
arguments against our involvement in the so-called
Vietnam war. But I must remind you that the United
States is more polarized today than it was before the
President ordered troops into Cambodia. Surely you
must recognize, if your mind is not completely blown,
that the principle which you seem to feel is at stake
in Southeast Asia is less important than the continued
existence of the democratic republic of the United
States. Or do you?

Peace,
William P. Maloney
Chicago, Ill.

*Dear Mr. Maloney: a) Surely you realize that the Vietnam war had nothing
to do with riots more sundering by far than our own, that have taken place
in recent months and years in France, Spain, Mexico, Italy, and India? b)
Surely you realize that to the extent that Vietnam is the cause of our own
disquiet, that disquiet could have been dissipated by moving much much
more decisively against North Vietnam in 1965 and 1966? c) Obviously you
do not realize that that is what I and* National Review *recommended, back
before, when wondering which of us is mad, you came so close to arriving at
the right conclusion. Best, WFB*

August 25, 1970

Dear Bill:

Attached is a note from George Schlatter, the
producer of the television series *Laugh-In*, inquiring
about the possibility of your appearing on the show.

Because of the previous misunderstanding, I thought
it best to transmit the offer exactly as given to me.
Please let me know how you would like this handled.
Best regards.

Sincerely,
Ben Griefer
William Morris Agency, Inc.

To: Ben Griefer

From: George Schlatter
Subject: William F. Buckley

Elliot Wax and I are seated here in the bowels of
Burbank going over a list of people we would like to
have appear on next season's Rowan and Martin's
Laugh-In. We had only gotten to the B's when I realized
it was time for us to make our annual proposal to
William F. Buckley. Recalling the series of somewhat
abrupt rejections these proposals have met with in the
past has in no way dampened our enthusiasm or lessened
our interest in Mr. Buckley.
  We would genuinely like for him to appear on the
show. We would give him approval of anything he would
say. We would in no way embarrass or humiliate him. We
promise not to book Gore Vidal to appear on the show in
any way during the forthcoming year. We will take out
no less than four subscriptions to *National Review*.
We will pay a fee of $1,000 plus all his expenses and
have him flown to California on a plane that only has
a right wing.
  I think we would have a marvelous time doing the show
and he could get off a number of beautiful "zingers"
of his own. We are all big fans of his. Although
occasionally some of the underlings on the show don't

agree with all of his viewpoints, we dig Mr. Buckley
and believe his appearance on *Laugh-In* would be fun
and his views would reach quite a large audience.

Please convey our request in a serious way to Mr.
Buckley because we would honestly like to have him on
the show. Please confirm.

Best regards,
George

Dear Ben:

How good to hear from you. In re Mr. Schlatter's kind and terribly
amusing invitation, my answer is no, notwithstanding the admiration
I feel for his program. I would rather be a comedian than a teacher,
but it was not meant to be, and by dressing in the robes of the former,
I diminish my usefulness as the latter. I hope Mr. Schlatter understands.
At any rate, please give him my best.

As ever,
Bill

Dear Mr. Buckley:

Ben Griefer forwarded your letter of June 2nd, in
which you politely but firmly once more rejected our
annual invitation to come to Beautiful Downtown
Burbank.

I am writing to you in hopes of changing your mind. I
mean, now, let's face it Bill . . . in a few minutes you
could strike a blow for conservatism here in the very
midst of our little hotbed of liberals, cuckoos and
questionable characters of all persuasion. . . . (If
you have a minute would you be so kind as to punch up
that last sentence for me? I somehow feel I could have

been more articulate, more humorous and more persuasive.) Onward.

In an effusion of enthusiasm, we will agree to the following restrictions: We will submit all material to you in advance and tape only the remarks that you find amusing. We will let you know in advance how each line will be used and what will precede and follow each comment. We will publicize it as much or as little as you wish. We will agree to not bother you again this season. We will give you a photograph, suitable for framing, of each cast member reading *National Review*, or not reading it, whichever you prefer. We can, if you wish, include a few serious remarks (and with the exception of Dr. Billy Graham, we have never deliberately done that before).

I will not bore you with a lot of logic as to the effectiveness of such an appearance; however, some people credit Mr. Nixon's appearance on *Laugh-In* as one reason for his victory. Some people credit us . . . others blame us, but we do have an enormous audience and through humor we can make some important comments and observations. Naturally, anything of your own that you would like said could be included.

We try very hard on *Laugh-In* to present both sides of issues and to limit our humor to fair comment. We try to do a "put-on" not a "put-down." We satirize and comment humorously, but without anger or venom. We do not take sides or present the personal political views of the people involved in the show. In this way we try never to become a platform of anything other than a good-natured, well-meant voice, presenting a humorous look at our society and the people and issues of importance.

It is always much easier to find humor in the anti-Establishment approach and to make jokes about the Administration and its leaders. There is also much humor in the opposition's viewpoint, and since we are committed to presenting both sides, we feel that we could do this best with someone of your stature, charm and wit.

Incidentally, let me point out how much easier it will be on all of us if you immediately agree to appear and thereby avoid the necessity for more letters and even perhaps personal embarrassment as peculiar characters in strange garb accost you and yours in public places offering exotic enticements in a spectacular manner.

In conclusion, while I do not feel that my personal integrity as an individual should constitute any element of this appeal, I do promise to vote any way you want, now and for evermore.

Best regards,
George Schlatter

Dear Mr. Schlatter: You win. Yours exhaustedly, WFB

December 1, 1970

THE VICE PRESIDENT
WASHINGTON, D.C.

November 12, 1970

Dear Bill:

My sincere congratulations on the Fifteenth Anniversary of *National Review*. The growing popular acceptance of the magazine and the ideas it has come to represent are a tribute to the tenacity and dedication that you and those who have been drawn to you have displayed over the years.

Please extend my best wishes to all attending your celebration this evening.

Sincerely,
Spiro T. Agnew

THE WHITE HOUSE
WASHINGTON, D.C.

October 26, 1970

Dear Bill:

The growth of *National Review* during these past fifteen years must surely be as gratifying to you and your staunch associates as it is to the many Americans who look forward eagerly to each new issue. You have every reason for pride in these years and for great satisfaction in accomplishments both eloquent and honest.

With style and imagination, you have done a great deal to fill out the spectrum of current political thought for all of our country's citizens. *National Review* has not been afraid of controversy, and the stimulus you have given to public debate has been a healthy one for every member of our society. I am especially pleased to have this opportunity to send to you and to each member of the editorial board and staff my best wishes for future years of lively and successful activity.

With warm personal regards.
Sincerely,
Richard Nixon

January 26, 1971

August 25, 1964

Memo to: WFB
From: Gertrude Vogt*

I have been asked to pass this message to you from the
American Federation of Television & Radio Artists--you
cannot appear on any more radio or TV recordings
unless you become a member of AFTRA.

September 1, 1964

Dear Mr. Groot [AFTRA Executive Secretary]:

Would you be kind enough to tell me what membership in AFTRA
involves, whether I am free to join or not join according to my desires,
and what are the sanctions used against me in the event I should opt not
to join? . . . WFB

September 3, 1964

Dear Mr. Buckley:
. . . membership in AFTRA involves the completion of a
membership application and payment of the applicable
initiation fee of $200, and semi-annual dues of $15
for the first dues period. Since AFTRA has a union
shop in all of its collective bargaining agreements,
it is necessary that persons who appear on radio or
television, in AFTRA-covered employment, be members
of the American Federation of Television and Radio
Artists within the period prescribed by law. In such
cases, all of the minimum terms and conditions of the
applicable AFTRA Code or contract would prevail, . . .

---

*My first, and longtime, personal secretary.

September 22, 1964

Dear Mr. Groot:

In the light of the fact that I have apparently no alternative than to join your union, I shall proceed to do so, under protest. Would you be kind enough to send me the application form? Wm. F. Buckley, Jr.

October 20, 1964

Dear Mr. Sage [AFTRA]:

You have now asked me to promise to abide by the constitution of the union without ever letting me see a copy of the constitution. Would you kindly send me one? Wm. F. Buckley, Jr.

November 3, 1964

Dear Mr. Sage:

Now that the television series I was to have hosted has been canceled—without the public viewing of a single one of the programs—do I assume that you no longer require me to join your union? Please advise.
Wm. F. Buckley, Jr.

November 4, 1964

Dear Mr. Buckley:

In answer to your letter of November 3rd, please be advised that you are still required to be a member of AFTRA, although the television series which you were to have hosted has been canceled and has not been broadcast. . . . send me a fully executed application for membership with your check in payment therefor. M. Sage

November 6, 1964

Dear Mr. Sage:

I do not know why it is so difficult to get concrete answers from officials of AFTRA, but I shall patiently try once again to get some. I would like to know:

1) Why am I now being required to join AFTRA even though I am not appearing any more frequently than I have any year during the past ten years on radio and television? 2) Is it my understanding that I would not be allowed, if I were a member of AFTRA, to appear on programs free of charge, which is what I do most often? 3) Do you require others who appear irregularly on radio and television, and who do so primarily to disseminate a point of view, to join AFTRA? For instance, is Congressman John Lindsay a member? Is [New York Conservative Party Chairman] Kieran O'Doherty a member? Is [ACLU Chairman] Roger Baldwin a member? 4) Why do you persist in sending me an application form which asks me to "apply" for membership in AFTRA, when the actual situation is that you are requiring me to join? 5) Assuming that by the exercise of sheer force you are in a position to deprive me of what some might consider my constitutional right to speak my mind on programs to which I am invited—by, for instance, calling a strike against any producer who invites me—are you prepared to accept a payoff: I.e., can I simply send you a check for whatever sum of money you exact as tribute, and spare myself the humiliation of joining an organization I do not wish to join? Wm. F. Buckley, Jr.

January 1, 1966

Designation and Application for Membership in the American Federation of Television and Radio Artists New York Local. 1) I hereby apply for membership in [AFTRA] and agree to be bound by each and every provision contained in the Constitution . . . and by any and all by-laws, rules, regulations, orders and resolutions of the Federation and the Local whether now in force or hereafter enacted. I agree that the said amendments, by-laws, rules, regulations, orders and resolutions are binding upon me as of the date of their lawfully taking effect, regardless of the rights, if any, vested in me prior to such date. 2) I hereby designate [AFTRA] as my exclusive agent for collective bargaining purposes in any and all matters dealing with the radio industry, television . . . 3) I authorize my employer to deduct from my compensation my dues, assessments and obligations or portion therefore to [AFTRA] . . . 5) Enclosed herewith is $ _____
Signed _____

November 23, 1970

Memorandum from William A. Rusher to WFB

   I asked Mr. Lewis [of AFTRA] . . . what would happen
if Buckley were to withdraw from membership in AFTRA as
a matter of principle. Mr. Lewis replied, cordially
but firmly, that "principle" can also be spelled
"principal," and that it would not be in Mr. Buckley's
interests to withdraw, since in that case AFTRA would
instruct WOR-TV (with which the union has a contract)
to stop broadcasting *Firing Line*. He went on to say
that AFTRA has similar contracts with every other
television station in New York City, so that (in
effect) *Firing Line* could not be broadcast . . . at all.

New York, January 12, 1971—William F. Buckley Jr. filed suit today challenging the constitutionality of a requirement that he join and pay dues to a private organization or be denied his right to work on the public airwaves. (The announcement was made at a press conference this morning in the Overseas Press Club.)

The suit was filed in the United States District Court, Southern District of New York, by Mr. Buckley and National Review, Inc. against the American Federation of Television and Radio Artists (AFTRA) and RKO General, Inc.

The formal complaint states that: "The requirement that plaintiff Buckley be a member of defendant AFTRA, pay dues and obey orders as a condition of his continued employment in the television and radio industry and the threatened denial of his access to television and radio stations place an unreasonable restraint upon plaintiff Buckley's right of free speech, deprives him of his property without due process of law, and breaches his rights under the First, Fifth and Ninth Amendments of the Constitution, which Amendments guarantee to the individual citizen freedom of association, thought, speech and political action, freedom to pursue the occupation of his choice, freedom from unwarranted invasion of privacy, and other fundamental personal and private rights."

At the press conference Mr. Buckley said: "The requirement that an individual pay dues to a private organization in order to work is a modern writ of indenture; the requirement that he do the same in order to express an opinion over the public airwaves involves an act of coercion by a private organization operating under government sanction.

"What is involved here is a fundamental civil and human right. And unless this country has lost hold of its reason, the Supreme Court will acknowledge, as I am confident it will, the right of the individual to exercise his rights as guaranteed under the First Amendment, even if he declines to join a union.

"Many of the people in the country labeled as 'liberals' eloquently object to any compromise of the individual rights of the citizen against the government—particularly free speech and privacy. I think it is time they join me in demanding that the individual have a right to join or not join, to pay dues or not pay dues to a private organization without surrendering his right to speak.

"I expect formal and informal support from other analysts and commentators and critics who use the broadcast media. I shall welcome them to join me in this lawsuit as co-plaintiffs. Who they will be remains to be seen, but I do know that for instance Sander Vanocur is opposed to compulsory union membership for newsmen, as is Frank McGee. Eric Sevareid recently emphasized the importance of press 'freedom from any and all attempts by the power of government to coerce it in any way,' which is precisely what the National Labor Relations Act has done, if its provisions are taken by unions as authorizing the restriction of free speech. Walter Cronkite has expressed his general concern with control, intimidation, and harassment of speech, and has said that 'we must fight tenaciously to win through Congress and the courts guarantees' of our freedoms. I cannot believe that he is unconcerned over attempts by private organizations to abuse the First Amendment by corrupting the law.

"I hope that these gentlemen, and others, will join me. And I invite the American Civil Liberties Union to declare its solidarity with us." Mr. Buckley said that he had already accepted an offer of legal assistance from the National Right to Work Legal Defense Foundation, which was organized to help American citizens assert their legal and constitutional rights when menaced by compulsory union arrangements.

March 9, 1971

Dear Mr. Buckley:

I wonder if, in your early life, an epinasty occurred in your brain. A great pity, if so, because you seem to have been meant for better things than reactionary polemicizing.

Sincerely,
Chet Cohen
New York, N.Y.

Dear Mr. Cohen: Yes, my epinasty happened when I was twelve. Until then, I used to look tropistically straight up into the sun, and was blind. Cordially, WFB

April 20, 1971

Dear Mr. Buckley:

I am a first grader. Teacher reads *NR* to us every day after nap time. The man who wrote from Antarctica said he was polarized.
Does this mean he was bit by a polar bear on the ice?

Anxiously,
Jimmy Jones

Dear Jimmy: If you are a first-grader, I will eat your teacher. —WFB

Dear Liege Lord,

  Help. I've fallen in love with the leader of the revolution at my high school. What do I do?

Loyally,
Glenda L. Warren
Brookville, N.Y.

Spy on him for the FBI and send us copies.—WFB

May 4, 1971

Dear Priscilla:

  A sample of the fan mail we receive. I look forward to reading Bill's reply.

Cheers,
Jackie [Sec. to Sen. James L. Buckley]*

[Enclosed:]
Hon. (?) James L. Buckley
Washington, D.C.

Sir:

  Now that my nausea has subsided after accidentally observing your appearance on *Laugh-In* last evening, I, as one of your constituents and former admirers, am constrained to comment.

---

*My sister Priscilla was managing editor of *National Review*. My brother Jim was elected junior senator from New York on the Conservative Party ticket in 1970.

Your silly grin as the inane and vulgar questions
were asked and your equally inane replies were less
than worthy of a senator of the United States. The
fact that you appeared on that program at all was an
insult to the decent people whom you represent. The
disgusting episode in which you freely participated
and apparently enjoyed as an accomplice in lending
your position to a disgraceful program is an affront
to the dignity of the Senate, to your family, to your
church, and to your constituency. I trust that your
acting the clown insured the support of the addicts of
the program who undoubtedly enjoy its indecencies.
I trust, too, that they are in the minority.

Yours,
Robert Hitchcock
Buffalo, N.Y.

Mr. Robert Hitchcock

Sir:

  I have forwarded your letter to my brother the
columnist--William F. Buckley Jr. It was he, not I, who
appeared on *Laugh-In*. I can't help but be curious as
to why you consented to watch a program of which you so
strongly disapprove.

Sincerely,
James L. Buckley
United States Senate

Dear Mr. Hitchcock:

  It is typical of my brother to attempt to deceive his constituents. It was,
of course, he, not I, who appeared on *Laugh-In*, just as you suspected.
On the other hand, you need not worry about it. His greatest deception

is as yet undiscovered. It was I, not he, who was elected to the Senate. So you see, you have nothing to worry about. You are represented in the Senate by a responsible, truthful man.

Yours,
Wm. F. Buckley Jr.

June 1, 1971

Dear "Senator":

  Your communication with Mr. Robert Hitchcock anent his confusing you with Brother James has caused a good deal of local amusement here in Buffalo.
  Mr. Hitchcock is No. 2 man in the oldest of the highly respected law firms in this city. He is a "very well informed" man who offers dicta on all matters, rightly or wrongly. To be thus caught with his pants down is most humiliating, and to find himself the butt of your humor is even worse, especially when I, personally, saw fit to post the article on the bulletin board of one of the better clubs of which Mr. Hitchcock is a member. The hilarity has become contagious.

Anon.

Mr. A. M. Rosenthal
New York Times
New York, N.Y.

Dear Mr. Rosenthal:

  On page 1040 of the *New York Times Almanac*, directly under "Buchwald, Art, [See page] 600," I find the entry, "Buckley, James L., [See page] 29." Under "Buckley, James L.," there is no "Buckley, William F., Jr., [See page] 600." However, on page 600, directly under "Buchwald, Art," appears the name "Buckley, William F." Now what I want to know, Mr. Rosenthal, is this: if Buchwald, Art, merits "[See page] 600," why does not Buckley, William F., Jr., merit "[See page] 600"? Or are you beginning, at the back of the book, to eliminate all "ruthless night-riders of the political right," and have merely failed (for lack of time?) to carry through Operation Vaporization into the front of the book? I was so incautious as to say, at a recent press conference, that I had rights that Bob Hope doesn't have. Are you perhaps applying the contrapositive of that declaration, to wit that Buchwald, Art, has rights that Buckley, W., doesn't have? More of this, Rosenthal, and I'll have you back writing headlines, at the execution of which you are a demonstrated expert.*

Yours truly,
Buckley, William F., Jr.
[See page] 600, 1971 Edition

October 8, 1971

Dear Mr. Buckley:

It is only after much soul searching that I have decided to relinquish my conservatism and join forces with liberals. After so many years. I want to get rid of those Communists under my bed and replace them with J. Edgar Hoover. And to prove I am just as broad-minded as any liberal, I am not canceling my subscription to *National Review*.

Mrs. T. G. Meulenberg
New York, N.Y.

---

*A *Times* editorial had used the "ruthless night-riders" line about my brother Jim during his Senate campaign. . . . Two weeks before the election, *NR* had used a spoof *New York Times* front page for our cover; Abe Rosenthal sent us a detailed mock-serious critique of our headlines.

Dear Mrs. Meulenberg: Don't feel bad. It's called "invincible ignorance," and you can get away with it under the circumstances. Don't forget the term: invincible ignorance . . . —WFB

November 5, 1971

Mr. Herb Caen
c/o *San Francisco Chronicle*

Dear Mr. Caen:

I have been sent two of your columns, dated June 7 and June 17.

In one, you write: "In fact, it was Jim, not Bill Buckley, who first cracked classically on election night: 'If I win I'll demand a recount.' "

In fact, it was Bill, not Jim Buckley, who made the crack; not on election night, but in mid-May, on announcing the selection of his running-mates.

In the other, you write: "For a nightcap, drop in at Elaine's, that amazing hangout for the literati on Second Avenue, and find Gay Talese, David Halberstam, Michael Arlen and Peter Maas and his lovely sad-eyed wife, Audrey. (It was to Audrey that Bill Buckley said, 'What is the secret behind those sad eyes?', departing hastily when Audrey replied, 'It is the sadness of a socialist looking at a fascist Republican.')"

In fact a) I have never laid eyes on Mrs. Maas, so far as I am aware, b) I have never said to anyone, "What is the secret behind those sad eyes?", and c) if Mrs. Maas or anybody else proffered such an explanation to me, her trouble would be not sad eyes, but black-and-blue eyes.

Yours faithfully,
Wm. F. Buckley Jr.

Dear Mr. Buckley:

June 7 and June 17??? Our Pony Express service is really slowing down. Or up. I really can't recall what I said yesterday, let alone last June, but since I have

been wrong before, I plead guilty again. It's what I
get for cribbing all my items from *Women's Wear Daily*,
without credit.

You really wouldn't want to mess up Audrey Maas,
would you? She's nice, but it could be that her husband
talks too much. I certainly don't think you're a
fascist Republican or anything.

All best,
Herb Caen

P.S. I think "What is the secret behind those sad
eyes?" is a dandy ice-breaker.

Dear Mr. Caen:

OK, let it go. I'll probably publish my correction in *National Review*,
for the record, as they say. You make Mrs. Maas sound very attractive!

My best to you,
Wm. F. Buckley Jr.

November 19, 1971

To the Editor,
Newsday

Sir:

I have just seen the letter you published by Mr. Louis Eackloff (April 23),
wherein he found it "unbelievable that *Newsday* continues to carry the
Buckley column. It persists in being full of fabrications, deceit and
intentional distortions. His article on Chile is a complete distortion. . . .
He completely forgets to mention his family's oil and mining interests
in Chile." Not only did I forget to mention my family's oil and mining
interests in Chile, my father forgot to tell us he had oil and mining interests

in Chile. But since we forgot we had them, it hurts us less that they should now be taken from us without compensation. I wonder, by the way, why Mr. Eackloff forgot to mention that [Chilean dictator Salvador] Allende is his father-in-law?

Yours cordially,
Wm. F. Buckley Jr.


```
Letters Department
Dallas Morning News
Dallas, Tex.

Sirs:

  Mr. William Buckley in his News column June 23 states
that he "cohabits comfortably with [H. L.] Mencken."
Thus by his own confession he is both a homosexual and a
necrophile. It's bad enough when the News runs a "comic"
strip by one Al Capp, charged on not one but three counts
with morals charges against young minor girls. When will
the News in all good taste begin to draw the line?

Very truly yours,
Edward Grimes
Dallas, Tex.
```

From the OED: "Cohabit . . . 1. To dwell or live together . . . 1601 F. GODWIN Bps. of Eng. 201 A certaine number of schollers to cohabite with the Cannons. 1667 SOUTH Serm. Ps. lxxxvii. 2 They were not able to cohabit with that Holy Thing [the Ark]. 1726 DE FOE Hist. Devil I. xi. (1840) 174 The wise and righteous generation that we cohabit with and among. 1809 KENDALL Trav. I vii 63 All that . . . do cohabit within this jurisdiction. 1971 BUCKLEY NR Vol. XXIII . . . cohabit most comfortably with Mencken in his insistence that the government is the natural enemy 'of all well-disposed, industrious and decent men.'" Grimes, baby, I'd hate to see your Rorschach test. —WFB

December 17, 1971

Dear Mr. Buckley:

I am a student at North Central High School in
Indianapolis. For a project I have to answer three
universal questions. I have to use *Great Books
of the Western World*, many newspaper and magazine
articles, novels, short stories, write letters, and
conduct several interviews.

This project counts 1/4 of my semester grade. As you
know, universal questions can only be answered by
opinion, and I would greatly appreciate yours.

1) Why is there war?
2) How far out does the universe go?
3) What happens after you die?

I would value your opinion highly. Thank you.

Sincerely,
John Mallinson
Indianapolis, Ind.

Dear John: 1) Because people disagree. 2) Twice half way. 3) I will go to
heaven. I don't know where you will go. —WFB

December 31, 1971

Memo to: C. H. Simonds*
From: WFB

Who had does not contract to "who'd." *He has* does not contract
to "he's."

---

*NR's assistant managing editor.

Memo to: WFB
From: C. H. Simonds

Subject: Lines to the man who succeeded, after sixteen years of education had failed, in teaching me the difference (I forget it just now) between "which" and "that"; and who has just called yet another failing to my horrified attention . . .

> What'd I do widout Buckley?
> He's wonderful—really, he's swell!
> If he wasn't here, who'd do that voodoo
> (Or voo'd who?) that he do so well?
> When I "who'd" where I'd ought to've "who had,"
> When, seized by the sleazes, I "he's,"
> A missive descends
>   (It never offends);
>   I never defend
>   But promise to mend;
>   To avoid future howlers I brush up on Fowler's—
> But way down deep I mourn Bill's actions:
> He lacks the courage of my contractions.

Dear Mr. Buckley:

I beg to let you know that on your *Firing Line* show which featured Miss Efron and Mr. Rooney, which was aired November 22 in Miami, Florida, you mispronounced the word "aposiopesis."

Yours sincerely,
Arthur Proner
Ft. Lauderdale, Fla.

A-po-SIGH-o-pe-sis is out. They're all saying, these days, a-PO-syo-pe-sis. Ask anybody. —WFB

January 21, 1972

Memo to: Jim McFadden, Promotion Department, *National Review*
From: WFB

My beloved colleague:

It is embarrassing enough to read drooly accounts of my published
works in the promotion pages of the magazine of which I am the editor;
I have for years been made aware of the necessarily hyperbolic nature of
promotional prose, and have with exemplary docility permitted my
works to be likened to the great masterpieces of the Western world;
I am not in the least opposed to quoting samples of my wit and wisdom
in said advertisements;
HOWEVER:
When, as on page 1453 of last week's issue, you give as an example of
that wisdom a fifty-word passage of prose which not only did I not write,
but I BURLESQUED in my book, words spoken not by ME but by
RAMSEY CLARK, all I can say is:
National Review has been infiltrated. —WFB

WFB: Proves my main point: "'*Cruising . . . Speed*' [is]
an . . . incredible . . . book." --JPM

My Dear Child:

Re your decision to ignore completely William
[Kunstler] [Nov. 5, p. 1258], I quite understand your
motivation. However, before you cut off all lines of
communication you might cite, to William, chapter and
verse from my best-selling Book, i.e., Ecclesiastes,
chapter 10, verse 2.

Truly yours (and vice versa),
God

P.S. Should you wonder why I get in touch with you through the U.S. Postal Service (I could, of course, have simply sent along this missive via thunderbolt), the truth of the matter is that I really do, as someone (I forget who) once said, "work in mysterious ways."

But I must go; Gabriel has misplaced his trump and I must help him find it. (This is, in fact, the third time he has lost it. That's three no trump!)

P.P.S. Looking forward con mucho gusto to meeting you in the not-very-near future.

Memo to WFB [from Research Director Agatha S. Dowd]: "The verse you asked for reads: 'The heart of a wise man is in his right hand, and the heart of a fool is in his left hand.' What a divine idea! --Aggie"

March 3, 1972

Memo to: God

Dear Sir:

What with Gabriel going down on three no trumps and You losing Your memory, things seems to be in a bad way up there.

It was I who said You move in a mysterious way, as any Episcopalian knows.

Talking of mysterious ways, fancy my having to reach You care of Bill Buckley.

I have the honor to be, Sir, Your most obedient servant,

William Cowper

March 17, 1972

Dear Sirs:

Re "Notes & Asides," Dec. 31: "*Who had* does not contract to 'who'd.' *He has* does not contract to 'he's.'" ??? If, as I suspect, "good English" comprises, inter alia, widely accepted locutions that would not cause the linguistically sophisticated instinctively to recoil, and "bad English" those that would (e.g., "he flaunted all the rules"; "he is one of those people who does . . . "; "Charles' book"; "the spitting image"; "he inferred in his letter that he would arrive next week"; "he said that, very soon, that he would make an announcement . . . "; "he used to always and emphatically say that . . . "; etc.), then I think you are wrong about "he's" and "who'd." "He has got the whole world in His hands"? No! "He's had too much to drink"--yes; "he has had too much to drink" is awkward and unnatural in conversation. "He's been here for a week"--sorry, I don't recoil. Unless "I've" (as in "I've had enough, thanks"), "We've" (as in "We've been looking all over for you"), and "You've" (as in "You've changed quite a bit") are not part of our language, then, surely and logically, "he's" is a proper contraction for "he has."

"Who'd ever heard of Pearl Harbor before December 7, 1941?" "He's the man who'd warned us of it long before it happened." OED to the contrary notwithstanding, my not-entirely-insensitive ear is not offended by these sentences.

My failure to cite dozens of additional examples of the proper use of "he's" for "he has" and "who'd" for "who had" should be regarded as merely aposiopetic.

With best regards,
Robert J. Cahn
New York, N.Y.

Correct. I should have said, "does not normally contract to he's." —WFB

March 31, 1972

Dear Bill:

Your letter of March 6 has reached me, and it was with regret that I learned of your decision not to serve another term on the U.S. Advisory Commission on Information.

I have deeply appreciated your service on the Commission for the past three years, and I have valued highly your contributions to its work. Your generous comments about the members of USIA and your associates on the Commission are gratifying and I know they would want to join me in expressing warmest thanks and good wishes to you.

Sincerely,
Richard Nixon

April 14, 1972

Dear Bill:

Three cheers to Dr. Ross Terrill. He slashed you to bits as you have been doing to yourself for the past year. Cancel my subscription.

Wm. W. Morris
Green Valley, Ariz.

Dear Mr. Morris: Cancel your own goddam subscription. Cordially, WFB

KENNEDY CURES CANCER, WFB COMBS HAIR

May 1972–September 1979

T HE NOMINATION OF George McGovern by the Democrats in 1972 was in many ways anomalous. McGovern's admirers (I came into this camp only years later, and at a personal level) believed adamantly that he had a good chance to be elected in 1972, though from the time of his nomination, something always went wrong. I remember a huge affair, a benefit for the New York Public Library, at which I contended against Professor John Kenneth Galbraith. He advanced the cause of McGovern, while I defended Nixon. The master of ceremonies was Art Buchwald. It was a week or two after Senator McGovern had dismissed vice-presidential nominee Thomas Eagleton, after a reporter had revealed that Eagleton had received shock treatment for depression. "The important question before the house," Buchwald spoke thunderously, evoking a predictable public reaction against incumbent Vice President Spiro Agnew, "is: Are we better off with a vice president who has been treated for mental illness or with one who hasn't?"

There was never, really, a plausible poll that justified Democratic confidence in McGovern's electability, yet it was clearly true that Richard Nixon was worried by what he considered a real prospect of defeat in November.

In seeking the opening to China—his visit there had taken place in February 1972—he was motivated by high statesmanship. But he worried that conservative voters would punish him for what we considered a net dilution of the anti-Communist spirit so ardently cultivated over the years—the price paid now for his endearments to Mao Tse-tung.

It was Mr. Nixon's determination to take advantage of every conceivable vulnerability of the contending camp that prompted him (acting through his top political adviser, John Mitchell) to authorize the Watergate break-in and even the raid on the psychiatric records of Daniel Ellsberg, the chief actor in the release of the Pentagon Papers.

Reductionism forswears distinctions. The John Birch Society was the great institutional organ of the fallacy that you can reliably infer subjective intention from objective consequence (we lost China to the Communists because people in government wanted to lose China to the Communists). The weakness in the reasoning of Robert Welch, Birch Society founder, was identified and conclusively repudiated by *National Review* back in February 1962. But hyperbole was pressed also in antipodal political quarters: in 1972 we received a notice to the effect that I had been "indicted" for "war crimes." Public "trials" would be held in Los Angeles, prosecuting me and a few others (including Henry Kissinger and Robert McNamara). Nut-time, yes. But even intellectually conscientious people can produce extremist analyses, and Mr. Nixon's opening to China stimulated a lot of this kind of thing. I attempted to correct Stanley Karnow of the *Washington Post* on this score, when what seemed like everyone in the country was attempting to explore, often fancifully, the impact on foreign policy of Peking's admission to the U.N.

Criticisms of *National Review* and of its editor were sometimes exuberantly personal. "The convincer in my decision to quit buying *NR* was the disgusting appearance of Editor Bill Buckley on TV with his seedy-looking Schickelgruber-Beatnik hairdo and sloppy-collared shirts, along with a retinue of whiney-snively-militant-Sodomite-looking punks." Pretty personal, that, no? Or, from a slightly different organ pipe, "You make me sick! I've never heard a person I'd like to shut up as much as I would you. . . ." Others at *NR* got solid tastes of the same, and recorded here are several references to publisher Bill Rusher that suggest ways he might serve as a surrogate "cult hero," to take the heat off the editor-in-chief. This series was kicked off by the bout of exhilarating exhibitionism from Stanley Michael Matis of Jefferson, Massachusetts, which he later repented.

"Notes & Asides" continued to be useful for stray purposes. I published my challenge to the *New York Times* Travel Section, which had grouped me as among "People [Who] Are Afraid of Flying": "My problem (since you are apparently interested) has been in the other direction. . . ." There was my provocative exchange with an official of the United States Advisory Commission on Information, concerning a radio set that the Commission had, I mistakenly thought, given me. And Clare Boothe Luce, at the time the most glamorous widow in town, weighed in deftly on the question, When is a woman a lady?

In the outside world, Nixon was now gone, supplanted by Gerald Ford. Each of them wrote to us from time to time. The editor of the *New York Times* wrote jocularly about *NR*'s expressed kinship with the Lord: "Could we send a reporter to see you to find out how God feels about a number of other things?" . . . And one of Professor John Kenneth Galbraith's spies spotted me on my sailboat, stuck aground off Menemsha. The author of *The Affluent Society* used his own equivalent of a Peeping Tom satellite to track the movements of the enemy.

❧

May 12, 1972

Dear Mr. Buckley:

Your article is just silly. You conservatives lose all credibility when you make such ridiculous exaggerated statements such as "not one word on the applicability of our principals of self-government and independence to the people of Taiwan" or "he toasted the bloodiest chief of state in the world." What principals of self-determination are we dedicated to for the people of Taiwan?

There are certainly many right-wing and left-wing dictators who are bloodier than the leaders of China.

Shame on you, you know better than that.

Sincerely,
Wylie F. L. Tuttle
President, Collins Tuttle & Co.
New York, N.Y.

Dear Mr. Tuttle: a) Name me a bloodier right-wing dictator than Mao Tse-tung. b) Please learn how to spell "principle." Yours faithfully, WFB

Dear Mr. Buckley:

a) Tutenkhamon, Timur the Lame, Herod, Caligula, King John, Louis XIV, any of the Popes in the sixteenth or seventeenth century, Ivan the Terrible, Franco, Salizar [sic], Hitler, Duvalier, the Internal Revenue agent in charge of my file, and the King of Zaïre. b) It seems to me it is not how you spell "principle" but how you apply yourself to them.

Wylie F. L. Tuttle
President

Dear Mr. Tuttle: As a purely factual matter, you are wrong. See, for instance, The Human Cost of Communism in China, *published by the Committee of the Judiciary, U.S. Senate, August 1971. To bring up Salazar in Mao's company is, really, not quite bright. By the way, it's Sal-a-zar. Cordially, WFB*

May 26, 1972

Dear Mr. Buckley:

  Did you see this, from the *Los Angeles Free Press*,
March 3?

Regards,
Irene Oliver
Los Angeles, Calif.

BUCKLEY INDICTED BY RIGHTIST YOUTH PAUL MUNGO

William F. Buckley Jr., noted conservative columnist and publisher of the *National Review*, was indicted last week for war crimes by a dissident right-wing group.

The group, Youth Action, from Washington, D.C., declared that Buckley, along with thirteen others, "did commit high treason, war crimes against humanity, and various other crimes and felonies against American youth and the American people as a whole. . . ."

A spokesman for the group announced they planned to hold a public trial of Buckley and the others, including Dean Rusk, Robert McNamara, Henry Kissinger, Henry Cabot Lodge, and both Nelson and David Rockefeller, in the Los Angeles area on Labor Day. An office would be opened in the county in July, they said, and at that time the exact location of the trial would be announced.

To SecDef Melvin Laird
Washington, D.C.

Dear Mel: Sometime before Labor Day, I'll be sending you a pair of targeting coordinates, and expect you to do your duty. —Bill

June 9, 1972

```
Dear Mr. Buckley:

  If it be true that resorting to the use of foul
language is the result of a poor vocabulary, what is
your excuse?

Sincerely yours,
Elevra M. Scorpio
Johnston, R.I.
```

Dear Mrs. Scorpio: Knowing just what word to use. Cordially, WFB

July 21, 1972

Stanley Karnow
The Washington Post

Dear Stan:

It doesn't really matter all that much, but I do have an archeological quirk that brings me to trace back such matters, so I am constrained to correct you. Perhaps you will not mind. After all, it is a little more comfortable to know that such enormities as you imputed to me were the result of misunderstanding. Better than that I should actually be saying, and thinking, such things.

You wrote (*Wash. Post*, Oct. 20, 1971): "In addition to Buckley's narrative, which warns Peking's admission to the UN 'will one day deliver the world to Mao Tsetung . . .' " I protested that I could not remember saying any such thing. You replied: "I think I quoted you in context and accurately, since I actually sat through the . . . film you narrated."

I have now come up with the script. Here is what it says: "Meanwhile, [i.e., as our new China policy goes forward] every day, hundreds of millions of people, enslaved by what Professor Wittfogel once identified as the megalomania of the aging despot, suffer and will suffer more from the knowledge that the United States, which sustained the dream of counterrevolution, has quietly given up; is showing the degeneration the Communist leaders promised their miserable people will, one day soon, deliver the world to Chairman Mao." Now: In your piece, you named Peking's admission to the UN as the effective agent that would deliver the world to Mao. Worse, you had me ascribing Peking's admission to the UN as the effective agent that would deliver the world to Mao. I, in my text, said that the *degeneration of the Western position*, which included the abandonment of any hope of counterrevolution, persuades millions of Chinese that their leaders are right, that the world will go to Communism.

I need not, Brother Stan, elaborate on the difference, beyond saying that the one statement is the statement of a madman, the other the analysis of

Your learned friend,
Bill

August 18, 1972

Gentlemen:

The convincer in my decision to quit buying *NR* was the disgusting appearance of Editor Bill Buckley on TV with his seedy-looking Schickelgruber-Beatnik hairdo and sloppy-collared shirts, along with a retinue of whiney-snively-militant-Sodomite-looking punks. David Susskind had more wholesome looking hangers-on.

I don't know exactly what has gotten into *NR* and Buckley, except that it repels me, or, to use a doperniggerism, "turns me off."

You convince Buckley to get a non-sloppy haircut, a clean, Perma-Press shirt with a non-comical collar, hire some clean-looking stooges for *Firing Line*, and--above all--cut out the four-letter toilet wall

and gutter language in *NR*. And review the sewer output
of the assorted media for what it is, rather than as a
praiseworthy "Emperor's New Clothes" phenomenon,
which identifies you as pseudo-intellectuals.

Until then, I'm not about to go slumming with
National Review.

Sincerely,
John R. Owen
Phoenix, Ariz.

Okay, Owen, come on back, and we'll use nice clean words, like you do.
Cordially, WFB

September 15, 1972

Dear Mr. Buckley:

In the introduction to your interview in the June
1970 issue of *Playboy* the magazine states that you, at
the age of six, wrote the King of England that it was
"high time" the English repaid American loans from
WWI. My grandfather made the remark that you must have
been quite an ass in your early age. My comment on the
subject was that this was an extremely laudable effort
demonstrating good sense. Who is right?

Sincerely,
John Prpich
Washington, Ill.

Dear Mr. Prpich: At age six, one is too young to be an ass. That came later.
Sincerely, WFB

September 29, 1972

Dear Mr. Buckley:

Of late you have come under strong attack from the
Washington Observer and a group which plans to try you
as a war criminal, Youth Action.

The thrust of their attacks revolves around an
allegation that you "advocated the American invasion
of Libya and the mass genocidal forced expulsion of
the Libyan population into the waterless deserts of
North Africa." According to your detractors, it is
because "he had his sights on the oil of Libya."

As an avid *NR* reader, I have often heard these
accusations. Would you, at least for the sake of this
sixteen-year-old conservative, elucidate your readers
upon this matter and set the record straight?

Cordially,
Peter Blackman
Malibu, Calif.

P.S. I would very much appreciate it if you would
publish this letter inasmuch as *NR* readers and other
conservatives would be at last convinced as to where
you stand on this issue. Thank you.

Dear Peter:

I reply to your letter only because you are sixteen years old. A
company in which my family has an interest and which operates mostly
in Australia and New Zealand bought an option to acquire a share of an
exploratory lease in Libya held by an unrelated company, but the option
was never exercised and had been abandoned prior to the publication of
the article to which the *Washington Observer* refers. I never heard of this

option until I made an investigation after the *Washington Observer* asserted that the purpose of the *NR* article about Libya was to acquire oil royalties. The suggestion that in order to help a Libyan exploration in which a company managed by members of my family had already decided not to invest I would a) found a magazine, b) corrupt its directors and editorial board so as c) fifteen years later to publish an article by d) a man I never met who e) proposed military action against the government of Libya with the professed purpose of bringing order to the Middle East but with the true, hidden purpose of f) facilitating the above-mentioned oil exploration, is a causative sequence which Rube Goldberg would have rejected as a strain on the intelligence. Intelligence, however, is a disqualifying attribute for anyone who seeks to take seriously the commentary of the *Washington Observer*, a smut-sheet whose only organizing principle is a dull-witted antisemitism.

Yours faithfully,
WFB

Dear Mr. Buckley:

  On Aug. 31, 1972, you wrote in a column that a rabbi smiled on the phone. How did he do this?

Yours,
Jerry Lon

Dear Mr. Lon: Practice. Years of practice. —WFB

October 27, 1972

THE WHITE HOUSE
WASHINGTON, D.C.

September 18, 1972

Dear Bill:

This is the first opportunity I have had to express my
appreciation for the forthright editorial endorsement
of *National Review*. Your and [the editors'] confidence
and support will mean a great deal to me as we carry
our message to the American people in the challenging
days ahead.

I recognize that we have differences on some issues
but I know we agree on more. Beyond that, the differences
between my opponent and me on issues are as widespread
as you frequently point out.

With kindest regards and appreciation.

Sincerely,
Richard Nixon

November 10, 1972

The Honorable James L. Buckley
United States Senate
New Senate Office Building
Washington, D.C. 20510

Dear Jim:

Next month, I propose to pass through the ivory
gates of the Republic of Zambia for a 21-day period--
hopefully not my last 21 days.

It has come to my attention that our brother Bill has
been declared *persona non grata* in that shining example

of democracy; and it has further come to my attention that Bill publicly allowed as how, on the whole, he "would rather be banned from Zambia than have to go there."

Accordingly, on the off chance that our brother's unpopularity with the authorities there might wash off on me, I appeal to you for your aid in securing me the full protection which has been so gloriously granted by our State Department to vexed Americans wherever they may find themselves in trouble.

Consequently, would you be kind enough to dust off your Form Letter #3 and substitute for the phrase "one of our most illustrious citizens" the words "one of our most powerful witch doctors"? Armed with this and with the seal of your august office, I will dare to enter Zambia with my worries confined to elephants and lions.

Affectionately,
John [W. Buckley]
Sharon, Conn.

Dear Mr. Buckley:

We were all sitting around drinking beer when it occurred to us that we ought to ask you. We keep a large poster of you on the wall so that whenever the urge comes upon us we can walk over and chuck you under the chin. The question is, do you mind?

Yours truly,
Roy Heimbach
John Howard
Risa Dworsky
Davvy Fuller
Kathy Heimbach
Marie Zaytoun
Raleigh, N.C.

Yes I do. But you may kiss my hand, if you like. —WFB

December 22, 1972

UNITED STATES ADVISORY COMMISSION ON INFORMATION
WASHINGTON, D.C. 20547
OFFICE OF THE CHAIRMAN

November 15, 1972

Dear Bill:

A note from the Voice of America informs us that they provided you with a Nordmende receiver on a long-term loan basis when you first came aboard.

They have asked me to remind you that if you no longer use the set would you kindly return it to the Agency. Many thanks.

With best personal regards.

Sincerely,
Louis T. Olom

Dear Lou:

You advise me that Voice of America asks, do I still have the portable radio they presented me with during my residence as a Commissioner of your august institution, and if so, would I please return it; to which I reply . . .

Anxious to do my duty, I took the radio on my trip to the Antarctic in January. You may or may not be aware that smack on the magnetic South Pole is a colony of 27 Russians. They are there apparently conducting scientific experiments, pledged to reveal their findings impartially to the world's scientific community. I desired to establish whether the Voice of America has a program beamed to this important colony. On arriving there, together with Secretary Chafee, Senators Goldwater and Buckley, and lesser gentlemen such as myself, I lugged my radio into the underground shelter where the Russians live and work, and while pretending to toast to international comity with vodka and caviar, I surreptitiously twiddled the dial in search of a program beamed to the South Pole. I must confess that I did not succeed, although I cannot say that my investigation was exhaustive, because one of my Russian hosts, suspecting that my concern for my radio in the circumstances was extra-scientific, began singing the Song of the Volga Boatmen most raucously, making it impossible to pursue my search for a signal beamed to the South Pole.

On my return to McMurdo Station, I discovered that the insides of the radio had frozen solid. But I managed, in Hong Kong, to eviscerate the old and usher in the new, so that by the time I reached New Delhi, the radio was in perfect order, and served me greatly in passing along the news of the day to Ambassador Keating, whose reliance on Jack Anderson for the thrust of American foreign policy normally required him to wait as much as one week for his *Washington Post* to arrive in the diplomatic pouch.

I next used the radio at the meeting of the Commission in London, so attached had I become to it—rather to the concern of my colleagues, who didn't feel it was a prudent use of my time to monitor the Voice in London while the Commission was attempting to interrogate prominent English lords and journalists, but my notebook records that the Voice reaches London with great assurance, no doubt explaining the amicable relations between our two great countries.

And from there, of course, I went with the President's party to Peking, with my radio in hand—by this time we had become absolutely inseparable. You may have read that a Chinese band played "Home on the Range" at that first banquet in the Great Hall of the People. Well, actually, you have the Voice to thank. Because I was showing it off to the conductor, and remarking on the fine reception in Peking, when he thought to nudge the radio up against the microphone, suddenly drowning the entire Hall with the chorus of America's favorite Western song.

But this proved to be the final triumph of the radio. The next night, while my colleagues were listening to *The Red Detachment of Women*, I was instead, though sitting in the auditorium, happily monitoring the Voice—I had bought myself an earphone in Hong Kong, so that I could listen uninterruptedly, without disturbing my companions. Suddenly an

Oriental, with a fixed smile on his face, beckoned to me, politely but firmly, just at the moment when, on stage, Ching-hua was being beaten by a running dog. I was taken to a little office and interrogated. What was I doing? I said I was listening to my radio. They said: That isn't your radio, that radio belongs to the Voice of America. I said, Listen, goddammit, that radio was given to me by the Voice of America, the better to perform my duties for the United States Information Agency, and no running dog of a Communist can get away with the slur on my country that when the Voice of America gives a Commissioner a radio, that radio still belongs to the government—we're not Communist yet, said I triumphantly. At this point they called in the Chief of the People's Security Service, who said abruptly: "Our operatives inform us that that radio is still considered to be the property of the United States Government. Since it was made quite plain to all correspondents that they could bring to China only their personal property, your radio is herewith confiscated."

So you see, it wasn't my fault. If Voice had told me it was still government property after it was handed to me, I certainly wouldn't have exposed it to all those risks. Perhaps you can ask Henry Kissinger, on his next visit to Peking, to plead with the People's Security Service to return it?

With deepest apologies,
Wm. F. Buckley Jr.

January 1, 1973

Dear Mr. Buckley:

To answer your question, no, I do not like your new cover design.* I rarely find a break with tradition to be an aesthetic improvement. I would rather buy Esso gasoline than Exxon; I would prefer to ride the Canadian

---

*Until the format change, the words NATIONAL REVIEW took up the top quarter of the cover; now the logo NR (with NATIONAL REVIEW in small type below it) appeared in the upper-left-hand corner.

Pacific Railway rather than the CP Rail; and I do not
regard the Fidelity Bank as a pleasing substitute for
the Fidelity-Philadelphia Trust Company. Avenue of the
Americas is still Sixth Avenue, and no conjoint NR is
going to replace *National Review* in the minds of right-
thinking Americans.

Sincerely,
Frederick Miller III
Philadelphia, Pa.

Dear Mr. Miller: We are still *National Review*. The contraction is for
convenience' sake, on the odd cover. Drop by next time you come to
Nieuw Amsterdam. Cordially, WFB

February 16, 1973

Is it true that you gave orders to your editors that the
American Party ticket was not to be mentioned throughout
the campaign, in the pages of *National Review*? If so how
much did it monetarily profit you personally?

Anon.

Dear Anon: No, it isn't true. I have only given one order to the editors
recently, see below:

MEMORANDUM

December 18, 1972

To: Priscilla, JB, Jeff, Linda, Kevin, Alan, Joe, Pat, Carol, Chris,
    Barbara, and George Will
From: WFB

Two things. We are suffering at *NR* from an epidemic of exclamationitis.
Two issues ago, in the review of Garry Wills's book, I was quite certain that

Will Herberg would succumb from it before finishing the review. It is a dreadful way to go. In the current issue, Mrs. Nena Ossa concludes her interesting essay on Chile, "That would be the moment to pack and leave!" "That would be the moment to pack and leave." is, I submit, a much tenser way of suggesting that that would be the moment to pack and leave. A few pages later, Herr Erik von Kuehnelt-Leddihn, discussing the economic situation in Spain, remarks that "it is significant that workers who had gone abroad are now coming back in large numbers because wages (for the skilled!) have become quite attractive." Why ! ? (Or, if you prefer, Why?!) The reader had nowhere been led to believe that Erik had constructed his argument in order to mock the superstition that unskilled wages were attractive in Spain. So why? I ASK YOU, WHY!

The other thing. A ukase. Un-negotiable. The only one I have issued in seventeen years. It goes: "John went to the store and bought some apples, oranges, and bananas." NOT: "John went to the store and bought some apples, oranges and bananas." I am told *National Review*'s Style Book stipulates the omission of the second comma.

My comment: *National Review*'s Style Book used to stipulate the omission of the second comma. *National Review*'s Style Book, effective immediately, makes the omission of the second comma a capital offense!

March 16, 1973

Dear Mr. Buckley:

About your un-negotiable Style Book ukase: Fowler says the comma before the "and" is considered otiose (his word). Too many sections.

Seventeen years of silence, then the ukase labored and brought forth a comma, by caesuran section no doubt. That indeed is exclamationitis!

Yours,
Vox Dictionarius
c/o George Foster
Los Angeles, Calif.

Dear Vox: Otiose blotiose. He dreamed of conquering Guatemala, Panama, San Salvador and Nicaragua. Without the comma, San Salvador and Nicaragua appear positively zygotic. Is that what you want, Vox? Well, count me out! —WFB

March 30, 1973

BAKER, NELSON & WILLIAMS
COUNSELORS AT LAW
20 EXCHANGE PLACE
NEW YORK, N.Y. 10005

February 27, 1973

Re: Buckley & Evans v. AFTRA

Dear Bill:

Judge Brieant has signed the judgment which we proposed. By its terms he declares:

"Those provisions in any 'Code of Fair Practice' or other collective bargaining agreement between defendant and networks, broadcasters, stations, and other employers in the television and radio industry requiring, or purporting to require, that plaintiffs continue to be members of defendant, pay dues to defendant, and/or comply with defendant's orders and regulations, as a condition of the production or broadcasting of the programs *Firing Line*, *Spectrum* or other program on which plaintiffs Evans and Buckley may appear, are void and of no effect as to plaintiffs, and, further, plaintiffs Buckley and National Review, Inc. may continue to make and sell the package show *Firing Line* and plaintiffs may continue to appear on television and radio as they see fit irrespective of

continued membership in defendant, the payment by
them of dues, or their compliance with defendant's
regulations and orders, all without harassment or
interference by defendant."

He stayed the judgment during the pendency of any
appeal and allowed us costs.

Sincerely yours,
C. Dickerman Williams

*Viva Williams. Viva Brieant. Viva the National Right to Work Legal Defense
Foundation.* —WFB

April 13, 1973

Dear Mr. Buckley:

I have occasion to write to thank you, at the risk
of being over-dramatic, for possibly saving my life
or at least saving me from serious injury. My latest
spate of Buckley consumption consisted of *Cruising
Speed*, in paperback, and *Inveighing We Will Go*, read
in the weighty hardbound version and originally
procured from the Base Library of the U.S. Air Force
Base at U-Tapao, Thailand, where I recently spent two
weeks on detachment. This is how you came to save my
skin. On the occasion of one rare afternoon off during
those two weeks, I was relaxing in a lounge chair
outside my quarters, sunning and reading. I was
eagerly progressing through an early chapter of
Inveighing when just to my right, about six feet away,
or well within striking distance, a medium-size dreaded
King Cobra--for which Thailand is famous--raised its
head to leer at me. I assume my chair must have
been in his favorite path of travel or something, but

I knew I couldn't leap from deep within that
comfortable chair faster than he could travel that
six-foot distance, if he chose. Being careful not to
betray my intentions, I tensed to toss your book at
him as we stared each other down. I flung it and
rocketed from the chair, not bothering to see if I
hit him. At a safe distance I stopped, turned and saw
the reptile slither into some bushes a safe distance
away. Yes, I could have been reading anyone's book
at the time, but it was your book, and aside from
its excellent content, I am extremely glad you
wrote it!

Sincerely, and with great admiration,
Philip Allen Keith
Lt., Patrol Squadron SIX
FPO San Francisco, Calif. 96601

*Dear Lt. Keith: Thanks. But why didn't you just try reading aloud to the
cobra? Regards, WFB*

July 20, 1973

Dear Mr. Buckley:

   Tch-tch--you'll never learn.
   I don't really mind your dipping into your pathetic
little treasury of Shakespeare quotes--the effect is
nice and you don't overdo it. But, please--get them
right. On page 622 of *NR* (June 8), you reply to a
letter from reader S. Manning with the most threadbare
of your quote stock, thus: "Dear Mrs. Manning: That
would be gilding the lily. Yrs. cordially, etc.," and
that rumbling sound you've been hearing ever since is

ol' Bill Shakespeare spinning like a top. Ol' Bill
never said anything about gilding the lily, and
were you playing hookey during the term they taught
King John?

Act IV, Scene 2, Earl of Salisbury in reply to Earl
of Pembroke:

> Therefore, to be possessed with double pomp,
> To guard a title that was rich before,
> To gild refined gold, to paint the lily,
> To throw a perfume on the violet,
> To smooth the ice, or add another hue
> Unto the rainbow, or with taper light
> To seek the beauteous eye of heaven to garnish,
> Is wasteful and ridiculous excess.

Did you get any other letters on this? Or am I the
only Shakespearean hawkeye among your readers?

Cordially,
Saul Glemby
New York, N.Y.

*Dear Mr. Glemby: 1) To call to the attention of anyone over 14 that
Shakespeare didn't say "gild the lily" is like calling to the attention of anyone
over ten that Voltaire didn't say the one about how he would fight to the
death for your right to say it. Come to think of it, I doubt very much that
Voltaire would fight to the death for the right of anyone to remind anyone
that Shakespeare didn't himself use the phrase "gild the lily." 2) The phrase
"gild the lily," and a number of other phrases, can be used even though
Shakespeare did not originate them. 3) When we use a cliché around these
parts, boy we mean to use a cliché, understand, Glemby? 4) Of the four
editors of* National Review, *one used to teach Shakespeare, one still does,
and, when I retire, I intend to. Cordially, WFB*

August 3, 1973

Memo To: The Editors
From: Bill Rusher

You will recall that at lunch WFB told me that the correct version was "And makes us rather bear those ills we have / Than fly to others we know not of." Attached hereto is a photostatic copy of page 81 of the "Yale Shakespeare" edition of *Hamlet*. I call your attention to line 82 of the Shakespearean text, and to the fifth word on that line.

Of course, people who gild lilies can hardly be expected to boggle at omitting "that"s. I do, however, encourage those of you who are hereafter gently put down by our Editor to make your own independent investigation. Besides, strictly in terms of the rhythm, I prefer Shakespeare's line to Buckley's.

Memo to: Bill Rusher
From: WFB

Indignor quandoque bonus dormitat Homerus, ass.

August 17, 1973

Memo to: The Editors
From: Bill Rusher

Buckley Contemplating a Bust of Rusher

He's got me! In Shakespeare I never could shine
Or boast of my varsity letter.
What wormwood, to catch my erroneous line!
(What gall, to say Shakespeare's was better!)

I'll frame a riposte with a confident ring
That will seem, to my public, to flatten—
Concealing somehow that it does no such thing . . .
I've got it! I'll put it in Latin!

WAR: *Where would you put it?* —WFB

August 31, 1973

Dear Bill:

The enclosed is for your attention. --JKG

[Enclosed:]
John Kenneth Galbraith
Professor of Economics at Harvard University
Cambridge, Mass.

Dear Mr. Galbraith:

I have been a fan of yours for quite some time and
I agree almost 100 per cent with your liberal views.
I particularly enjoy watching you chew up William F.
Buckley during debates.

I would like to ask a favor of you. I possess a hobby
and that is I collect autographs of people I admire. I
would appreciate it very much if you would send me your
autograph and I will be very grateful. Thank you and
best of luck to you in the future.

Sincerely,
Mark Sheeran (Age 14)
New York, N.Y.

*Dear Mark: You are at the perfect age to be a fan of Professor Galbraith. He
has a new book coming out and with every copy you get two popsicles. Watch
for it. Forgivingly, WFB*

October 12, 1973

Editor
The Travel Section
New York Times

Dear Sir:

I have only just now seen your spread of August 12, under the heading "Some of the Best People Are Afraid of Flying," and featuring a gallery of faces including what I hope is the most poltroonish photograph of me ever taken. The writer includes me in the roster of the fearful with the sentence, "William F. Buckley says in his typical fashion that flying is 'committing an egregious effrontery upon the laws of nature' and recommends 'a little of the grape.'"

I have great respect and sympathy for those who fear to fly, but it happens I have never been one of them. The snippets quoted by the author are from a column of advice to the airlines for the benefit of those who fear to fly, and the recommended poultice is of course pleasant not only for them but for others.

My problem (since you are apparently interested) has been in the other direction. As a student at Yale, I, along with a law student who came to be the sainted junior senator from New York, and one or two others, purchased a secondhand airplane. I found it so exultantly easy to fly, after a single 45-minute lesson, that I volunteered in a moment of characteristic compassion to fly a fellow student to Boston the more quickly to unite him with his lady love. I managed to take off all right, and to land, but on the way back to New Haven I quickly deduced that I had forgotten to account for the previous night's return to Eastern Standard Time, leaving me short of light by one hour. I ended by flying one hundred feet above the ground over the NYNH & Hartford railway, which brushed by the airfield at New London, mercifully lit: and I effected my first solo landing, and hitchhiked back to school. Since then I have patrolled the DMZ [in Vietnam] in a light plane, engaged in a night mission over Laos in a low-flying DC-3, chased kangaroos in Darwin in a helicopter, flown upside down in a Phantom II at twice the speed of sound, taken the controls of a helicopter to do a pas de deux with Barry Goldwater Jr. over the Antarctic, glided serenely in a sailplane over the presidential palace of Salvador Allende, and suffered the rebuke of the pilot for trying to take the controls while landing on an aircraft carrier in the Gulf of Tonkin. My observation is correct, that the laws of gravity are offended by flight, but what else is new? The laws of truth and beauty are likewise offended by the First Amendment's guarantee of freedom of the press, and who would compare, unfavorably to the airplane, the disaster record of the airplane over against, let us say, that of the *New York Times* editorial page?

Yours cordially,
Wm. F. Buckley Jr.

Mr. Herbert Kenny
Boston Globe
135 Morrissey Blvd.
Boston, Mass. 02107

Dear Herb:

The weekend is not entirely over, so perhaps I shall still hear from you, Frances Bronson having reported that you intend to call. I hope you will, and that you will have cheerful news to report.

Since you are the culture editor of your august paper, perhaps you would convey these words to Mr. Brendan Malin, your television critic, who reviewed my program with Michael Foot. Mr. Malin writes: "Argumentative when he should be inquisitive, Buckley might have done some incisive interviewing but his role was to extinguish more than extract the views of Michael Foot. . . . Next time Channel 2 is hosting an international celebrity it should look elsewhere for an interviewer."

But you see, *Firing Line* is not designed as an interview program. It is specifically (i.e., it's in the contract) described as an exchange of opinions, between me and my guest. It has been so for only seven years, which may be the reason Mr. Malin hasn't yet learned that that is the formula.

More. Mr. Malin writes: "When it comes to international affairs, the microphones of the world should be closed in the verbal evanescence of William F. Buckley." Now I do not mind Mr. Malin's opposing my views on international affairs—that much I glean onomatopoetically by running Mr. Malin's prose through my lips.

But I do mind being made the implicit victim of sentences that simply don't make sense. It is impossible to conceive of a microphone as being "closed," or "opened," any more than you can "close" or "open" a switch. I do not know what "in the verbal evanescence" means, though I know what "verbal" means, what "evanescence" means, and, until reading Mr. Malin, thought I knew what "in" meant.

And then how terribly vexing to him that ten days after Mr. Malin should seek to "close" the microphones of the world to—a free translation—my views on international affairs, I should have been designated by the President as the public member in the United States Delegation to the General Assembly of the United Nations. Every time I open my mouth, in the months ahead, before that considerable microphone, I shall say to myself: Remember, Bill, your words are charting the future of Brendan Malin.

I shall accordingly speak in language intelligible and, as is my wont, will utter only noble thoughts.

As ever,
Bill

November 23, 1973

Dear Mr. Buckley:

Hey, this is a curious thing, and I thought you might wanna hear about it. Anybody's welcome to be a right-winger, ain't they? But if you're a YOUNG one, people figure you gotta be a Bill Buckley hero-worshipper; it's

like a CULT!! I had a subscription to *National Review*,
but they kicked me out of the factory on account of I
kept drawing rabbits on the shipping cartons, so now
I can't afford to keep it alive. Don't it seem sometimes
like people are watching *Firing Line* mostly because
they like the way you talk and do stuff with your face?
Then you go on Johnny Carson's show and he kills 15
minutes telling you you've got a good vocabulary; I
realize he doesn't get paid for getting into deep
theoretical goo, but don't you think maybe your style
overrides the substance of what you're saying?

But that's not all bad; for example, with Bobby
Kennedy, I thought a lot of what he was saying in 1968
was pretty bizarre, but he was such a charmer that I
probably would have voted for him in November. That
doesn't say much for my mind, granted, but it just
shows that people like me can get sidetracked very
easily, and . . . uhmmm . . . I think if I was you and
I was trying to say important things and everybody was
getting mesmerized by my voice, that'd be both spooky
and flattering. I probably wouldn't mind, because I'm
basically superficial, and I'd be too busy soaking up
all that public attention to really care . . . but you
seem to believe what you're saying, and I should think
you'd get spooked and bothered.

Anyhow, what I got to thinking is this: If there's
gotta be a right-wing cult hero, why don't you make it
Bill Rusher? If you could get everybody honked up on
Bill Rusher, get all the impressionists to do Bill
Rusher routines, and get him to ride a motorcycle and go
to Truman Capote's parties and everything, maybe then
when you come around people will listen to what you say
and wait for him to come raise his eyebrows at them?

But this is coming out wrong, because I'm making it
sound like nobody takes you seriously. That isn't what

I'm getting at. But I do think it'd be a good idea to
make Bill Rusher a cult hero, and I think he could pull
it off! . . . and then if your brother decided to try
for the White House he wouldn't have everybody saying,
"Look, it's Bill Buckley's brother . . ."; oh God, now
I'm getting that wrong, now it sounds like they don't
take *him* seriously.

   Forget it. Anyhow, I like what you've been up to, as
much of it as I understand, and I'm gonna subscribe
again as soon as I get another job. If I said anything
bad here, I didn't mean to.

Best wishes,
Stanley Michael Matis
Jefferson, Mass.

*Dear Mr. Matis: We are training Mr. Rusher. Keep your eyes on him, but
keep it quiet. Cordially, WFB*

December 7, 1973

Memo to: Bill Buckley
From: Bill Rusher
Re: Progress report on turning me into a cult hero.

   It's a mixed bag. Frankly, I'm getting discouraged.

   1. The eyebrow bit. For various obscure
physiological reasons, my eyebrows simply won't go up
high enough. I can wiggle my ears, especially my right
ear (pure coincidence--no symbolism intended), but I
doubt the gesture would be visible on television at a
distance of more than six inches.
   2. The Bill Rusher sweatshirt. I have located a
manufacturer who would be willing to turn out a gross

of these at a ridiculously high price, but then
who would wear them? One of my godsons--a likely
purchaser--has told his father that the kids on his
block have threatened to beat him up if he wears a
Bill Rusher sweatshirt.

3. Truman Capote simply refuses to return my phone
calls.

4. On the other hand, I am getting so I can twiddle
a red pen almost as well as you can. It's rather like
baton twirling, right?

5. I have set myself to learn one new big word
a day. This week so far, for example, I have learned
prevenient, susurrant, and dichotomous. But maybe
we're wrong to try such slavish imitation. Perhaps
I should develop my own shtick in the language line:
e.g., use only one- and two-syllable words, or try to
become famous for a lavish use of French profanity.
In short, maybe the more dichotomous the better (see?).

6. I flatly refuse to ride a Honda. For one thing,
they're dangerous in this Manhattan traffic. For
another, I live only three and a half blocks from the
office, so it isn't necessary. If you really think some
unique mode of transportation is essential to the
image, I can rent a Shetland pony from a stable up
in Westchester, but you'll have to keep it here at
the office.

Really, instead of trying to turn me into the new
cult hero so people will take you seriously, it might
be better if we reversed our strategy and tried to sell
me as an anti-hero: i.e., a guy so irredeemably square
that he becomes famous for it. I am sure I could do it;
I think people might buy it; and it would be a hell of a
lot easier on me.

December 21, 1973

Dear Mr. Buckley:

I still can't believe it! I was innocently walking down *NR*'s street today, looking hopefully for lights in a certain office window just as I always do, when suddenly, through a burst of sunlight, a red, white, and blue rainbow appeared, and the music of Bach's *Magnificat* filled the air. Then, who should I see but the new RIGHT-WING CULT HERO, BILL RUSHER!

He wasn't riding on a Shetland pony or a Honda, or passing out free copies of *National Review*, or anything like that--he was just WALKING DOWN THE STREET. I think he may have mumbled some irreverent French words at being recognized, but I was too flustered to pay attention to anything he was saying. I mean, it isn't every day I hear Bach on 35th Street and bump into a REAL CULT HERO, wow!

Sincerely yours,
Judith H. Block
Bronx, N.Y.

January 4, 1974

Dear Mr. Buckley:

I read somewhere that you don't send out Christmas cards. Okay--and you can whistle before I send you a Christmas card. Lex talionis, as you would say.

Regards,
Ella F. Winter
Chicago, Ill.

Dear Miss Winter: I am sorry; but I recognize the merit of your point. Merry
Christmas. By the way, the law you cite was repealed by the gentleman
whose birth your Christmas cards celebrate. Cordially, WFB

January 18, 1974

Dear Mr. Rusher:

Now that your cover has been blown, we are having a
more difficult time executing the final phases of Project
Superstar: The Selling of Rusher. Subsequently, we have
moved from the loft into a warehouse, and burly guards
are dissuading the curious.

The sweatshirts have just arrived. The "Thrill with
Bill" motto is less pronounced than we expected (i.e.,
needs more speckled silver in the lettering), but Peter
Max's likeness of you in an ascot with a devilish grin
turned out just right. The kids in Peoria will eat it
up. As for the buttons, we took your suggestion and
used both slogans, dark grey letters on a light grey
background: "Don't Mess With Bill" and "No More Mr.
Nice Guy." The matchbooks and plastic wine glasses
bear a like color scheme. (By the way, the Agency
called concerning the "action ads." Since someone has
already used the harpsichord thing, we think it
appropriate if you would learn the saxophone.)

Bill Haley and the New Comets are doing the number we
talked about. And we are up to our ears in volunteers
for the Rusherettes. Yes, I know you strictly said,
"No groupies!" but what can I say? With this kind of
campaign you have to expect these things. I understand
Glen Campbell has the same problem. He might give you
some pointers.

Finally, we have a man at NBC who has given PBS the
go-ahead for the Special. It will be a one-hour deal

scheduled for next fall with you leading a singing choir of small children on a walking tour of the Upper East Side. I'll have more by the next planning session. (As usual, please leave the money with the laundry woman at Chi Ling's on East 36th and Lexington. Thanks.)

As ever,
Ron Docksai
Chairman, Young Americans for Freedom

April 12, 1974

Dear Mr. Buckley:

 I don't see how you qualify to discuss things like the oil scarcity or high prices. Presumably these don't get in the way of your ski vacation in Switzerland. You make me sick.

A. L. Llevyleld
Los Angeles, Calif.

Dear Mr. Llevyleld: The assassination of Caesar didn't get in my way but I can discuss it. And there is no way to get away from higher prices. They have risen in Switzerland more than in the U.S. During my "ski vacation," I wrote 24 columns, did television programs in Dublin, London, Johannesburg, Salisbury, Nairobi, and Dakar; did a documentary in South Africa; wrote a book on the United Nations; and answered 500 letters, most of them, happily, less unpleasant than your own. —WFB

May 10, 1974

Dear Mr. Buckley

 Unfortunately your brilliant intellect is inside your head and does nothing for your male beauty. You are, shall we say, unhandsome. This misfortune does not confer the right to appear disheveled.

A decent respect for the opinion of mankind (of conservatism, if not B.B.) would require that you mitigate nature's failure where reasonably possible.

Toward that end, I enclose a pocket comb. If you ply the instrument faithfully I shall consider contribution toward a haircut.

Don't mention it!

Charles L. Murphy
Tarzana, Calif.

Dear Mr. Murphy: I have combed my hair. What do I do now? Cordially,
WFB

June 21, 1974

To the Editor
The Editorial Page
The New York Times

Dear Sir:

You write (May 27): "There is something repugnant in the enthusiastic publicity-seeking of Senator James L. Buckley of New York in participating in a whaling expedition by the hunters of an Alaskan village."

Now I have seen everything. So my brother is visiting, once again, the Arctic circle. It is his fourth trip, not even counting his trip to the Antarctic. He has a thing about Arctic circles. He first went to the Arctic circle way before he went to the Senate, and he will go to the Arctic circle after he is out of the Senate, assuming the inconceivable, that he and the voters should tire of one another before death do them part. On this particular trip a *New York Times* reporter asked to go with him. Jim said okay, but only if the Eskimos say okay. Those who know my brother know that the prospect of a reporter traveling to the Arctic with him for the purpose of recording the Senator's movements, far from overjoying him, was a tribulation he bore gracefully only because he will bear the pains of Purgatory gracefully. A *New York Times* editor then decides to put the *New York Times* reporter's story on the visit on the front page, whereupon a *New York Times* editorial writer gives my brother hell for publicity-seeking! Your reference to his "gleeful pursuit" of a whale is both gratuitous and ignorant, inasmuch as my brother, a naturalist, has himself always declined to shoot or hunt down any living creature. What was he supposed to do while his hosts were shooting the whale? Cock his eyes heavenward and recite the De Profundis? I do not doubt the integrity of his concern for endangered species, though I confess that my own is qualified as I meditate a world without the species that writes *New York Times* editorials.

Yours faithfully,
Wm. F. Buckley Jr.

August 16, 1974

Dear Mr. Buckley:

"If Richard M. Nixon went to the basement of the White House and discovered the cure for cancer, the *Washington Post* would never take notice." --William F. Buckley Jr.

"If Ted Kennedy went to the basement of the United States Senate and discovered the cure for cancer, William F. Buckley Jr. would never, never, but never take notice." --Charles Cascio

Sincerely,
Charles Cascio
Scranton, Pa.

Dear Mr. Cascio: Wrong. I would give Senator Kennedy credit. But I would say it was a very clear case of serendipity—and take renewed interest in trips to my own well-stocked cellar. Cordially, WFB

November 22, 1974

Dear Bill:

In a recent column in which you recounted a chance
meeting in a broadcasting studio with J. K. Galbraith,
you wrote, quite in passing, that while you and the
economist were conversing a "lady theologian" was on
the air.

Reading that "lady" bit I was instantly reminded of
Archie Bunker.

All in the Family, as you know, is the Americanized
version of a popular British TV show designed to
caricature the Anglo-Saxon bigotries and class
prejudices of the lower-class Englishman, who is the
last-ditch defender of middle-class Victorian
attitudes.

Archie, the dock-walloper, like his British
counterpart, considers himself a member of the superior
race and sex. Archie is especially faithful to the
genteel nineteenth century tradition that a gentleman
is a man who refers to any woman who isn't obviously a
trollop as a "lady." Archie speaks of "lady cabdrivers,"
"lady cops," "lady short-order cooks." His gentlemanly
mark of respect for the "weaker" sex is, however, not
altogether unmixed with disdain and resentment. Archie
makes it quite plain--all in the family--that "ladies"
who try to do any "man's job" are really "amatoors" who
have no business to be in the business.

Even Archie's next door neighbors, the "Eyetalian
lady" and the "colored lady," cannot trifle with
Archie's masculine sense of racial and sexual
superiority without being instantly downgraded into
"that female wop," or "that colored female," who are
ruining the neighborhood. Archie seldom refers to a
woman as a "woman." This is probably because he views

women less as persons than as the reproductive and nurturing function of a manmade world, made for men. A "woman" is what goes to bed with a man, has his babies, and gets his food on the table. In Archie's sex lexicon the men are men, but women who are not "ladies" or "females" are "the girls" or "the wives."

Altogether, Archie is a crude but powerful master of what feminists today call "verbal sexism"--the patronizing putup or contemptuous putdown of women just because they are women. When Archie speaks of women in any social relation to men, he never puts them on man's level. For example, in Archie's world the women are sometimes permitted to bowl with the men. As Archie might tell it, "Us men give them female bowlers a good licking," or "Us fellers let the lady bowlers win a few offn us."

So permit me, dear Bill, as woman writer, former congresswoman, and former ambassador, to remind you that professional women today view the "lady" bit as a conscious or unconscious masculine putdown. And allow me further to suggest that my favorite man columnist (who is also a gentleman) should leave the use of "lady" as a sex classifier and/or gratuitous social status indicator of professional persons to the Archie Bunkers of the writing profession.

Affectionately,
Clare [Boothe Luce]
Honolulu, Hawaii

Dear Clare: Your point is clearly made, and magnificently advocated. Henceforward I shall confine my use of the word to such references as "lady wrestlers," where the oxymoronic imperative clearly prevails. Love, Bill

December 20, 1974

Dear William:

   Hi, my name is Frank McNamee. I'm in the seventh
grade. I'm a 86 student in Reading. I'm a Republican,
also, I watch *Firing Line*. It's cool. Do you know
what antidisestablishmentarianism means? My Brother
and Dad are successful business men. My dad is a
supervisor in M. A. Brudk and Sons. My brother is an
Assistant Manager at Beneficial Savings Bank. He says
he likes to be around money. He subscribes to *National
Review*. I have a hobby of writing letters to artists
and famous People like Yourself. I chose you out of the
President, and Milton Shapp. (He's one of them Demo's)
or (Radicals). People say I'm crazy for writing to a
famous guy like you. But I don't know. Where [sic] you
on the Yale Football team? Sir, I hate to bother you
but could I have your autograph to show my Democratic
Social Studies teacher please? Thank you.

Sincerely,
Frankie McNamee
Philadelphia, Pa.

P.S. If you decide that you will write to me Please
write Frankie because my Pop has the same name. And
I would like to open my own mail. Thank you.

Dear Frankie:

   *1) Yes, I know what antidisestablishmentarianism means, and I'm for it,
which I bet your Democratic Social Studies teacher isn't. 2) My Dad was a
successful business man too, but I'm not. I like to be around money too,
which makes me wonder what I'm doing at* National Review. *3) I am glad
you chose me out of the President, and Milton Shapp, and I don't think*

you're crazy for doing so, just smart, as your Reading score suggests. 4) No, I wasn't on the Yale Football team, but I was on the Yale newspaper. 5) I attach my autograph for your Democratic Social Studies teacher. Tell her please not to use it to register me as a Pennsylvania Democrat. What else do they teach you how to do at the Democratic Social Studies courses in Philadelphia?

Yours sincerely,
Wm. F. Buckley Jr.

January 31, 1975

Dear Mr. Buckley,

   I'm not a lover of *NR*'s cover.
   To say the most, it can't boast of the slightest
artistic merit one could ever hope to ferret out of
thin invention.
   That's not to mention that, to say the least, c'est
bougrement triste.
   While this land endures,

Faithfully yours,
G. A. Di Giovanni
Stamford, Conn.

Dear Mr. Di Giovanni: Then why don't you start on page 2, espèce d'idiot?
—WFB

February 28, 1975

Dear Mr. Buckley:

   Since watching your TV programs over two years, I
noticed your health has deteriorated. My 15-year-old
son admires your discussions with various guests.
I told him you are educated and intelligent but you

never learned a daily routine to keep your strength.
He wants to know if you were studious at his age and if
my advice will help you now.

Now for necessary habits you must develop in order
for everyone to enjoy your TV and newspaper thoughts:

1. Eat whole wheat bread or wheat germ or oatmeal
   daily.
2. Drink two glasses milk or eat 1/4 lb. pot cheese,
   buttermilk, or farmer cheese.
3. Order salads, carrots, string beans (green and
   yellow vegetables).
4. Eat potatoes, nuts, beans. The protein, oil, and
   fruits you most likely enjoy.

Besides good food, take a daily walk where there is
air and get to sleep before 12:00 or take a nap during
the day.

Sincerely,
Mrs. M. Feiner
New York, N.Y.

Dear Mrs. Feiner: Thank you for your advice. But you should know that one's "health," on television, is exclusively the doing of the makeup technician, who could not care less whether you have consumed a vitamin in years. A skilled technician could reverse the appearance of the two Dorian Grays. But I thank you for your wholesome advice, and will heed it, except that if I followed your second instruction, I would perish of whatever it is you perish from if you have too much cholesterol. Cordially, WFB

April 11, 1975

Dear Mr. Buckley:

I am a teacher with credentials in English, political
science, history, mathematics, humanities, and Japanese,

and yet I barely have the ability to decipher your
vulgar prose.

I can't recall ever having seen such an obvious search
for and display of archaic vocabulary and overall
obfuscation in an apparent attempt to be "the learned
one." You stink!

You are a complete joke, a pedant, a phony
conservative. You're an upstart. You may be a New
Englander and a Yale man, but, in no way do you have
the class of a Cox, a Richardson, or even a Kennedy.

Yours truly,
John M. Herlihy
Seaside, Calif.

*Dear Mr. Herlihy: Sorry. English, political science, history, mathematics,
humanities, and Japanese are not quite enough. But don't give up, Herlihy.
Don't ever give up. —WFB*

April 25, 1975

Dear Bill:

Somebody asked, specifically, so let me say it
directly: some of the best journalism in America is
being printed in *National Review*.

Just wanted you to know.

Sincerely,
Dan Rather
CBS News
New York, N.Y.

Dear Dan: Many thanks. —Bill

May 9, 1975

Dear Mr. Buckley:

Eight or nine months ago, while I was out of work, I got into my brother's whiskey and wrote you a partially coherent letter dealing with the idea of turning William Rusher into a cult figure . . . and then, five or six weeks later, my friend Buster telephoned to tell me that my note had turned up in *National Review*. It was quite a shock. I went to the library later that day and asked whether they had a copy on hand; the lady at the front desk kept telling me that I must have the name wrong. She said I was thinking of *The National Observer*, and finally she began to get terribly impatient. I figured I'd better leave.

The rest of the week was pretty difficult; I wanted to find out just what I'd written, but I couldn't find the magazine anywhere. The kid who works at Henry's said they only get two or three copies, some old Tory from Rutland buys them all, and none of my friends here in Jefferson go anywhere near anything but *Cycle World*; Leroy says I'm a queer for writing letters, anyhow. By Saturday it was getting very bad. Buster lives way out in Chicopee, and I didn't dare push the Plymouth that far; 109,000 miles on it, and the fan belt was slipping, so what I finally did was to put a call through to Buster and ask him to cut the letter out and mail it to me.

He did. I got it on Wednesday, and it was much worse than I'd suspected it could be. It was fey. I got to thinking that everybody would figure I was one of those characters who hang around campaign headquarters trying to impress the candidate. This kid sounds like Jack Ruby, they'd say; he brings doughnuts to the police station and pats people on the back.

The rest of the autumn was a time washed by second thoughts; I made an agonizing reappraisal of myself, decided the best defense against further incidents would be to stay away from spirits, put a big sign on the wall beside the typewriter: IF YOU'RE DRINKING DON'T WRITE. It works, too. Things began getting straight. They took me back at the plant after I promised to stop drawing rabbits, Leroy lets me borrow the Triumph on Sundays, and Buster never even mentions the letter.

Best wishes for a happy summer,
Stanley M. Matis
Jefferson, Mass.

Mr. Matis: You've made it a happy summer indeed. —WFB

August 1, 1975

Dear Mr. Buckley:

  As a long-time subscriber, more or less generous contributor, and sincere admirer of *NR*, I was terribly disappointed to read in "Notes & Asides" of the April 25 issue the laudatory remarks from Dan Rather. Where do you suppose *NR* went wrong?

Yours truly,
Joseph Voyles
Department of German
UC Berkeley

Dear Mr. Voyles: NR *never goes wrong. If Dan Rather likes it, Dan Rather went right. —WFB*

October 10, 1975

Dear Mr. Buckley:

   Upon the excuse of your most expert interest in
words, permit me to remind you that détente's primary
meaning in French is the trigger of a gun, and à la
détente translates as the act of pulling the trigger.
   Perhaps détente's secondary meaning of relaxation
derives from the calm which succeeds an accurate pull.

Sincerely yours,
C. Parkinson
Cleveland, Ohio

November 21, 1975

Mr. Max Frankel
Sunday Editor
The New York Times

Dear Max:

   Thanks for your note. . . . By the way, the misprint in my review in the
current issue threatens my reputation. Will your obituary in due course
refer to the departure from the scene of a renowned photographer?

Cordially,
Bill

Dear Bill:

   I always knew your reputation would finally be your
undoing. The order here is not to "fiddle" with your copy.
Therefore, when you wrote in the recent review of Dick
Reeves that Ford's "public support when down," it was

assumed by no fewer than 14 copyreaders that you were supplying some special stylistic touch and a most pregnant interpretation.

So you see we were guilty of nothing more than hero-worship, of which we would, of course, be delighted to be disabused.

Any other problems?

Best,
Max

Dear Mr. Frankel:

The late Mr. Buckley, before defenestrating, desired me to communicate to you that he when out fighting.

Yours truly,
Frances Bronson
Sec'y

December 5, 1975

Dear Mr. Buckley:

I am ten years old and have your picture right over my bed, next to that awful Figgy Calabrese who won't even look at me. I always watch your TV shows and I love the way you eat your pencils. I think you are very intellectual and should be next president of Connecticut. The reason I am writing, would you come and speak to my fifth grade class? They won't even let us say prayers here.

Love and XXXXXXXXX,
Mary McNally
New London, Conn.

Mary, my foot. I can tell when some cheap school principal is trying to beat
me out of a lecture fee. Get Figgy Calabrese. —WFB

PARIS WHITE HOUSE

NOV. 16

WILLIAM F. BUCKLEY JR.
NATIONAL REVIEW

AS FAST AS AIR FORCE ONE WILL FLY I WILL NOT BE ABLE
TO MAKE IT HOME TO PERSONALLY JOIN IN CONGRATULATING YOU
AND NATIONAL REVIEW ON YOUR TWENTIETH ANNIVERSARY. I
APPRECIATE YOUR KIND INVITATION TO SEE YOU LEAVE THE
FIRING LINE FOR THE RECEIVING LINE. AND I WILL MISS HEARING
YOUR DISTINGUISHED SPEAKERS, SENATOR BUCKLEY, SENATOR
GOLDWATER, AND GOVERNOR REAGAN. PLEASE NOTE THAT THESE
ARE IN ALPHABETICAL ORDER AND NOT NECESSARILY IN THE ORDER
OF MY HIGH REGARD. SERIOUSLY, I COMMEND ALL THE STAFF OF
NATIONAL REVIEW AND ITS ERUDITE EDITOR FOR PROVIDING
AMERICA WITH A SERIOUS, RESPECTED, AND RESPONSIBLE
CONSERVATIVE VOICE WHICH IS NOT ONLY MORE OFTEN RIGHT THAN
LEFT BUT ALSO MORE OFTEN RIGHT THAN WRONG. PLEASE ACCEPT
MY VERY GOOD WISHES AND WARM PERSONAL REGARDS.

GERALD R. FORD

December 19, 1975

Dear Mr. Buckley:

Since my last correspondence, we now represent one
of New York's major media-communications companies who
has a limit on escalation in their lease.
As a major space user, they were able to negotiate
this tenant oriented clause when escalation was not a

significant factor; their rental is also substantially
"below the market" for this modern uptown office
building.

   You can understand the value of this uncommon
clause; no landlord today would even consider it.

   I would be happy to discuss this unique situation
with you at your convenience.

Sincerely,
George E. Angel
New York, N.Y.

*Understand the value of this uncommon clause? Why my dear sir, I don't
even understand your letter! Cordially, WFB*

January 23, 1976

*In October 1975 I wrote a column on the difficulties of navigating through
the changing mores in forms of address. The column concluded:*

My bias, on the whole, continued in the direction of a tendency to for-
mality, so in the last few years I made a determined effort to overcome it,
wherein I came across my most recent humiliation. Mrs. Margaret
Thatcher was my guest on *Firing Line.* Rather to my surprise, the English
being more naturally formal than we are, halfway through the program
she suddenly referred to me, once, as "Bill." I declined to break my *Firing
Line* rule, and so persisted with "Mrs. Thatcher." However, the next day
when we met again at a semi-social function, I braced myself on leaving
and said, "Good-bye, Margaret." And a week later, writing her a note congratulating her on her performance, I addressed it: "Dear Margaret."

   Today I have from her a most pleasant reply, about this and that. But it
is addressed, in her own hand (as is the British habit: only the text is
typed): "Dear Mr. Buckley." Shocked, I looked at the transcript—only to

discover that, on the program, she was talking about a "bill" that lay before the House of Commons. The trauma has set me back by years, and I may even find myself addressing Johnny as "Mr. Carson" next time around. I suppose, though, that at fifty, the problem becomes easier in respect of the twenty-five-year-olds. At seventy it will be easier still. Well before then, I hope to be able to address Margaret, I mean Mrs. Thatcher, as Madam Prime Minister.

HOUSE OF COMMONS
LONDON SW1

Dear Bill,

Having just read your article in the *Washington Star* of 28th October, I have made my first New Year Resolution. From 1st January, 1976, Mr. Buckley shall be "Bill."

I shall assume the appropriate reciprocity.

Yours sincerely,
Margaret Thatcher

July 23, 1976

To the Editor
Playboy Magazine

Dear Sir:

Karl Hess, replying to your interviewer's question in the current issue of *Playboy* ("Although you admire Buckley, you no longer agree with him. From your point of view, where did he go wrong?"), answers: "He went wrong because, in the end, he actually believed he was preserving God's will. I remember a dinner party Bill had at his place in Connecticut soon after the first issue of *National Review* was published [twenty years ago]. This fellow kept staring at him and finally said, 'You know, Bill, you have the profile of a young Caesar.' Well, instead of being embarrassed by that preposterous remark, Bill reveled in it. And in retrospect, I conclude that people who do not blush when they are compared to Caesar end up being Caesar."

I remember the scene very well. You see, at my dinner parties I try to guide the discussion into profitable directions of common interest and substantial purpose. On the agenda that particular evening was the question: Does my profile more closely resemble that of Julius Caesar, Alexander the Great, or Rudolph Valentino? The argument raged for hours, and I attempted to be entirely dispassionate on the subject, believing as I do in untrammeled democratic authority. The guests were pretty well divided when one of them, with singular authority, announced that my profile is indisputably more like that of Caesar, and although I admit to a certain wistfulness at the rejection of Alexander and Valentino (a strong minority case can be made in their favor), I was secretly pleased that Caesar had won out. I thought I had kept my pleasure safely undetected. But I must congratulate Mr. Hess on his acuity. He saw through to my true attitude, even as now he has penetrated to the real intentions of God, the Founding Fathers, and Mankind.

Cordially,
Wm. F. Buckley Jr.

October 15, 1976

Dear Mr. Buckley:

An acquaintance inflicted the gift of a piranha with appropriate aquarium and paraphernalia on me. For six or seven months now I have had to put up with gurgling water, whirring motors, and the uneasy feeling that I am a potential meal. My office is so laid out that the aquarium is approximately four feet from a cupboard

wherein I store a television set. The piranha, named
Charles, seldom watched television, being far more
interested in reviewing whatever documents I happen
to be working on. However, on two occasions we have
observed Charles watching *Firing Line*. It is rather
obvious when the goofy fish is watching television, as
the television set is a foot higher than the aquarium
and the fish must position himself at an angle to
observe the screen.

Could this mean I have a fish with good taste?

Very truly yours,
Francis D. Papenfuss
La Crosse, Wisc.

Dear Mr. Papenfuss: That depends on who on the screen he wants to eat.
Cordially, WFB

October 29, 1976

Mr. Eric Sevareid
CBS-TV
New York, N.Y.

Dear Eric:

  Mr. Paul Sweeney, the associate producer of *Firing Line*, advised me a
week ago that your publisher declined, in your name, an invitation to
appear on *Firing Line* on the grounds—she represented herself as
quoting you—that "Mr. Sevareid is offended by recent writings by
Mr. Buckley about himself and about Teddy White." I called Teddy
White, and he told me that although he has very nearly total recall about
animadversions at cannot remember when he found my criticism
personally offensive. So much for Teddy. Now I sit here wondering what
I did to you. . . . Could it have been the column in which I disagreed with

your definition of "conservatism," as you gave it out to your listeners some months back? Do you have handy—I'd be pleased to consult it—a Guide to Permissible Criticism of Eric Sevareid? If so, I hope it contains a supplement listing the names of those of your friends any criticism of whom you do not tolerate. Since I criticize practically everybody, yet you name only Teddy White, am I to gather that only he enjoys your special protection? Or that he is your only friend? But that really is preposterous, because even I have always thought of myself as, among other things,

Your friend,
Bill

November 26, 1976

Dear Bill Buckley,

   I am referring back to your letter of September 20 on the matter of friendship. My friendship is not easily given or easily withdrawn and I have arrived at the age when nothing else is quite so important.
   But I'm afraid I take a view different from yours on permissible strains; and your logic confuses me. Because you have informed your many readers that Sevareid is not worth listening to I could not see why you would wish me on your TV hour.
   When you began your AFTRA suit I made a published comment in support. What followed were repeated sneers in your column because I chose not to join the suit. You did not inquire as to why, but implied, as I read it, that it was due to cowardice. If there is anything in the world that does not frighten me, it would be that union. I declined to join simply because my time, my health, and my money were already painfully overextended and because lawyers assured me the suit had no chance.

You have, I am told by a source I believe, publicly
described Teddy White as a national bore. If he chooses
to disregard that, it's his business.

Sincerely,
Eric Sevareid
CBS News

Dear Eric:

Concerning your letter, a few observations:

1. My friendship, by contrast, is easily given, but does not preclude
concurrent disagreement.

2. I do not remember telling my readers that you are not worth
listening to. And even if I thought you were not, I would not hesitate
to put you on *Firing Line* because people whose views are not worth
listening to are often listened to nevertheless. *Firing Line* has the
advantage of giving its guests an opportunity to test their views
under pressure.

3. I have indeed publicly pondered why you have not joined a lawsuit
which you approve of. You never inquired whether it would cost you
money to join me in the lawsuit to bring First Amendment protection to
news analysts on the airwaves. The answer is No. The National Right
to Work Legal Defense Foundation is defraying all expenses. Nor was any
investment of your time required. I do not see how the lawsuit would
have impaired your health, unless your nerves are shattered by bad
judicial decisions, in which case you are probably a nervous wreck
anyway. As for the lawsuit's having no chance, remember we won at the
circuit court level, and, despite setbacks, the case proceeds. Do I
understand you to be saying that you will not associate yourself with a
cause you believe will fail? How can you then associate yourself with so
hopeless a cause as Immunity for Eric Sevareid from Criticism?

4. I have not publicly or privately described Teddy White as a national bore, because I do not believe him to be a national bore. Indeed I have acclaimed in print, even while criticizing some portions of them, several of his books. Pray inform your Deep Throat that he is incorrect. Is he, by the way, the same source you regularly rely on when composing your news analyses?

5. "Dear Bill Buckley"! Oooo! Dear Eric, I fear that in that protracted tug-of-war between yourself and a terminal stuffiness, you have, finally, lost. And that is everybody's business.

Cordially,
Wm. F. Buckley Jr.

April 15, 1977

Dear Mr. Buckley:

But is conservatism fun?

Cordially,
Richard Chonak
Los Angeles, Calif.

Dear Mr. Chonak: Yes. But it's very hard work. Cordially, WFB

May 13, 1977

Dear Mr. Buckley:

I feel sure you will be enthralled to know that here at the University of Illinois, a once-great educational institution, the Office of Academic Affirmative Action has decreed that, vis-à-vis employment, "There shall be no discrimination because of physical or mental handicaps . . ."

How about that? Academic employment, too! Oh, I tell you, the ding-a-lings are taking over, and no mistake!

Best,
Sheila Jane Barnes
University of Illinois
Urbana, Ill.

August 19, 1977

Dear Mr. Buckley:

You are one of the leading conservatives in this country, but you wear your hair like a way-out liberal hippy. It is nasty looking, unkempt, and subtracts tremendously from your appearance. You would be a *fairly* good looking man if you would get a haircut-- not necessarily crew like your brother [Senator Buckley]. If you really are conservative, why don't you make yourself look like one?

With best wishes,
Sincerely yours,
Fellow Conservative
Greensboro, N.C.

Dear Fellow Conservative: If I were also good looking, don't you think it would all be just too much? Cordially, WFB

April 14, 1978

Dear Mr. Buckley:

This will acknowledge receipt of your letter dated January 18, 1978, in which you tender your resignation from AFTRA.

Your letter is a continuing manifestation of your campaign to attempt the destruction of any meaningful effort by a democratic union to achieve better wages and working conditions for its members. In all your writings concerning AFTRA you have never given any indication that you knew or had attempted to ascertain the enormous benefits that AFTRA has achieved for its members in the past forty years.

Your tender of resignation from AFTRA dated January 18, 1978, has been filed.

Sincerely,
Kenneth Groot
Executive Secretary
American Federation of Television and Radio Artists

Dear Mr. Groot:

1) Yours was not a democratic union until [co-plaintiff] Stan Evans and I made it so: membership in it was compulsory. 2) A lot of us value the First Amendment and the freedom of speech above the collective-bargaining benefits of any union. 3) I am happy when television and radio artists are well paid, but also I am unhappy when television and radio artists are out of work. That you achieve the former at the expense of the latter is widely suspected; I don't know: but that much is widely alleged, and is certainly true of a number of other professions dominated by the elite through the instrumentality of unions. And anyway, all of this leaves out the question, Why did you require us to spend $150,000, and seven years in court, to do what you now admit the law required you to do all along?

Yours faithfully,
Wm. F. Buckley Jr.

May 26, 1978

Dear Bill:

   After reading your fascinating novel *Stained Glass*,
my only regret is that I didn't appoint you as Head of
the CIA!
   What concerns me, as I am sure it must you, is what
the U.S. can or will do to counteract increasing
Communist subversion at home and abroad now that the
Congress and the Administration have castrated the CIA
and the FBI, as far as covert capability is concerned.
   Our mutual friend Whittaker Chambers must be turning
over in his grave.

Cordially,
Dick Nixon
La Casa Pacifica
San Clemente, Calif.

September 1, 1978

WHAT DO YOU PLAN TO DO THIS SUMMER? COULD YOU WRITE A
100-200 WORD ANSWER FOR OUR VACATION READING ISSUE? COPY
MUST BE IN OFFICE MAY 12.

HARVEY SHAPIRO, EDITOR
NY TIMES BOOK REVIEW

*[The italicized lines in the following letter were omitted in the version
published in* The New York Times Book Review.*]*

Dear Harvey:

   This summer I plan to do the usual things, plus something else.
I have elected to run the very serious risk of making a fool of myself.
How? You are obviously licking your lips. By trying to write a poem?

By undertaking a textual analysis of the speeches of President Carter? *By reading out loud editorials from the* New York Times? Worse. I belong to a club whose articles exact of its members non-demure participation in musical, dramatic, and cultural programs, and this year I have been asked to play the harpsichord at one of the evening events, as a small part of a variety show. I said: Yes, on the understanding that up until 24 hours before curtain time I may change my mind. I have selected a stretch of music that requires nine minutes for a performer of average competence to render, ninety minutes for such a performer to master. I shall be devoting every spare minute of my time during the entire spring and summer to the project, and will not know until the evening before whether I can go through with it. Is there a greater drama in the house? *Tell me, Harvey; and if so, run it bold, and hold the presses, and we shall all of us, your vast constituency, hold our breath. I'll let you know how it went, if it went.*

Best,
Bill

Mr. W. Parmer Fuller III
President, Bohemian Club
San Francisco, Calif.

Dear Parmer:

In the interval between the closing of the festivities on the Saturday night and my leaving the Grove, over a dozen members of the Bohemian Club approached me to apologize for the reception given by a few members to my appearance on the program. While most grateful to these gentlemen for their courtesy, I should like to record the following:

1. Although I undertook to play the harpsichord at the insistent invitation of Bob England, I withheld a final commitment to play it until Tuesday before the Saturday. On that Tuesday, I performed the 12

Mozart variations for Bob, in order that he might finally pronounce
on the advisability of playing before the large Saturday night assembly.
He reiterated his invitation.

2. I drafted, for submission to you, a few jocular sentences that might
serve by way of introducing my episode. In retrospect, I think I made a
mistake in failing to alert the audience that I intended to play seriously
(to the best of my highly limited ability) a piece which, while a musical
venture in childhood fantasy, is nonetheless a little masterpiece, and a
standard in the repertoire of many performing artists. I take full
responsibility for predisposing many members of the audience to think that
I was engaged in an elaborate sight-gag with music-box accompaniment.

3. I fully understand, under the provocative circumstances, the manifest
impatience of a few members, and, while appreciating the concern voiced
to me about their alleged inhospitability, I wish to advise you that I am not
in the least offended; that on the contrary I am grateful for the appreciative
response of so many Bohemians; and that I was greatly moved by your own
conspicuous generosity. At the risk of fulsomeness, I should add that such is
my affection for the Bohemian Club, and my respect for the resonant
gentility of its members, that my preternatural judgment of them would
probably not have been altered if they had mounted the stage for the
purpose of riding me out of the camp on a rail. Certainly I have no doubt
that W. A. Mozart would have done just that if he had been a member of
the audience. Although, to confess the dark side of my nature, I must admit
that if anyone had touched the harpsichord, I'd have killed, resigning myself
in my later years to cohabitation with Charles Manson and Patty Hearst.

4. In conclusion, I must share with you the utter joy I experienced
after the event on learning from a listener seated high among the
redwoods of his having overheard, shortly after I had begun, the
plaintive sigh from the listener behind him: "Vote No on Variation 13!"
Mozart knew when to stop, even if I have not learned when not to begin.

With cordial regards,
Bill

Dear Bill:

. . . As I left the stage that night, a sober Bohemian expressed to me his concern over what he called the rudeness of some members of the audience. I was confident that I was taking no chances when I assured him that you were not offended, but I'm glad to have your confirmation that my judgment was accurate. I like the idea of Bohemians doing something and doing it well outside the scope of their known skills. I also prefer Bohemian entertainment over imported performances, and you filled the bill.

As for the listener high in the redwoods, perhaps he, like Jerry Brown, is now in favor of Variation 13, having heard the applause.

Sincerely,
Parmer

February 2, 1979

Dear Mr. Buckley,

Gene Genovese, Editor of *Marxist Perspectives*, sings the praises of *National Review* as a model of popular political journalism. The efforts of those of us who work in the office of *MP* to keep track of the enemy would be aided by a comradely (whoops . . . collegial) exchange of subscriptions. I hope you will look favorably upon my modest proposal.

Cordially,
Jacques Marchand, Publisher
Marxist Perspectives
New York, N.Y.

P.S. Our list of subscribers includes several *NR* staff members. While I welcome such august converts, I assure you we have not yet placed moles in your organization.

Dear Mr. Marchand: If you have, you can fire them for incompetence. Cordially, WFB

February 16, 1979

Dear Mr. Buckley:

When I received my Dec. 22 issue of *National Review* (on Dec. 26, incidentally), I immediately turned to your "On the Right" and the "Trans-O-Gram."

I have heard you accused, at numerous times, of using long and obscure words and "usual dirty tricks with the English language" but assumed that these accusations were merely the fulminations of the semi-literate. This time, however, much to my surprise, I found it took less time to work out the "Trans-O-Gram" than to read your "On the Right," and with less use of my dictionary. Because I consider it to be futile to try to change your writing style, I am asking that you please arrange to have the "Trans-O-Gram" made more difficult.

Sincerely yours,
Richard I. Jackson
Sedona, Ariz.

Dear Mr. Jackson: My column in that issue was the "Trans-O-Gram." Cordially, WFB

August 3, 1979

Dear Mr. Buckley,

  You're the top--
  You're a balanced budget.
  You're the top--
  You're a New Left plummet.
  You're a bold swashbuckler whom nothing seems
    to daunt.
    You're a rebate payment,
      A tax derailment,
        You're the end of détente . . .
  (End of my problematic inspiration.)

Cheerio,
Henry Teichert
Oswego, N.Y.

Dear Henry: You forget—I am the end of the energy crisis! Cordially, WFB

September 28, 1979

Dear Bill:

  My article in *National Review* on some of the myths
of the American Indian aroused local ire. The student
council of the university, exercising that conscience
which we are called nowadays to yield to, voted to
censure me without even reading the disputed article. I
then received a threatening letter from D. Chief Eagle,
a survivor of the Sioux. I enclose a copy of my reply:
  "How!
  "White brother readum chicken tracks of red brother,
makeum paleface heart heavy; tears of sorrow flow all
over floor of teepee like great river.

"Lo, many moons ago Injun smokeum peacepipe, promise Great White Father puttum down tommyhawk, no makeum war forever more. Now me thinkum, *Injun speak with forked tongue.*

"D. Chief Eagle he says he invade white brother own hunting ground and castum lance at white brother. What kind talk this talk? Maybe D. Chief Eagle heap big silly humbug; maybe better watch out, you thinkum? White brother maybe lift up Injun hair pretty damn smart, hey? Maybe bury hatchet in D. Chief Eagle head, he come up here steal land, steal women. Makeum damn good Injun right quick, by Chrise.

"Ugh!"

John Greenway
Heap Big Chief Medicine Man
Professor of Anthropology
University of Colorado
Boulder, Colo.

Dear Bill:

I was fascinated to read today the column in which you reported your "feeling" that the Lord smiled on Andrew Young.

I have no way at all of disputing this. In fact my assumption, knowing you, is that you would not report a "feeling" without some pretty solid material to go on. Could we send a reporter to see you to find out how God feels about a number of other things? For instance, does He smile on our *Westchester Weekly*? This would be very important for our marketing people to know. We have a number of other important questions to put to

God about people and products He favors. Please let me know when all this can be arranged.

Sincerely,
Abe [Rosenthal]
Executive Editor
The New York Times

Dear Abe: I have a feeling the Lord will take care of the New York Times *on the eighth day. If in the meantime He weighs in more specifically, I shall pass along the information, always provided that what the Lord believes is fit to print. Yours cordially, Bill*

Dear Bill:

I write to tell you of a conversation I had yesterday morning on the ferry from Vineyard Haven to some place on the mainland in the general vicinity of Falmouth. It was as follows:

A man in plaid pants: "Did you know, Professor, that your friend William Buckley got stuck last night in Menemsha Channel? He was too far over to the side."

JKG: "It doesn't surprise me."

Plaid Pants: "What do you mean? I don't understand."

JKG: "William Buckley rarely gets anything right."

Plaid Pants: "I think that comment is unnecessary--and unkind."

My regards,
Ken [John Kenneth Galbraith]
Harvard University
Cambridge, Mass.

Dear Ken: Channel markers are not maintained by the private sector, whence the capacity to confuse. Cordially, Bill

Three

UP WITH TOM SELLECK, DOWN WITH COMMUNISM

February 1980–September 1991

I T WAS REAGAN TIME in the United States, and for *National Review*. He and I had been personal friends for years, and at *NR* we were political fans. But there was never any coordination attempted with his policy-making.

There was, in "Notes & Asides," a single episode of direct intercourse that had to do with his campaign. During the 1980 primaries I reminded the candidate of something President Carter had said to Rumanian dictator Nicolae Ceausescu; Reagan replied with an exact version of what Carter had said in Poland on the matter of the alleged independence of that satellite state. Meanwhile, one or two correspondents advised us that they too were running for president.

Although the Sixties and the Vietnam War were far behind us, student protest maintained its momentum. In 1980 the senior class of Vassar College invited me to serve as Commencement speaker, but the invitation generated such expressive protest that I withdrew. . . . And Ken Galbraith weighed in again, this time reminding me of my correspondence with Evelyn Waugh.

Criticisms and defenses, and counter-criticisms, on myriad topics of course continued. Mostly, the critics weren't public figures engaged in for-the-record reprimands or chastisements. But as far as we cared to establish, they had all given real names (no one feared retaliation for the sin of having criticized *NR* or WFB).

Just every now and again a quarrel was aired in the wider world, outside *NR*'s pages. There was an acerbic exchange at the center of which was syndicated columnist Mary McGrory. She was aroused by a news report that President Reagan had spent the weekend at the villa of Claudette Colbert in Barbados, from which he had sent out his weekly newscast. She wrote, "[Reagan] gave no indication of how he did his research. Did Claudette Colbert, his hostess, fill him in? Or was it his fellow guest, the millionaire columnist William F. Buckley Jr.?"

Mary and I could now go at each other with daggers drawn, after the disappearance from the scene of a figure important to us both—our joint syndicator, Harry Elmlark of the Washington Star Syndicate. We had mingled as his guests at two social affairs, and we saw each other again as fellow mourners at the funeral home. Now that Harry was gone, she could let it all out, and did. She was a fine writer, an adamant liberal, and a prize-winning reporter, dead in 1985 and, in the judgment of many of her newspaper clients, irreplaceable.

The Screen Actors Guild wanted to get into the act in the matter of a promotional ad acclaiming *National Review*. Objections were directed at Tom Selleck and Charlton Heston for doing extra-union work. . . . My own television program turned twenty years old in 1986, and critics were still, as they had done in the early years of the show, training on the host's shortcomings, which included his awkward on-screen posture—raising, however, questions about organic limitations to any attempt by me to oblige.

There was continued concern for language, maybe the only subject with which Art Buchwald, in his amiable see-it-all raillery, never concerned himself. He was always happily alongside, driving his Hertz car, an innocent smile lighting up his genial mockery.

And there was a lawsuit. With a single exception, we never courted lawsuits. I remember that when we began publishing, in 1955, we took out insurance. The policy was shrewd and specific. The company would protect us against adverse libel judgments up to $1 million, but a) would retain the option to suspend coverage if we didn't agree with a plaintiff's offer to settle; and b) would contribute no more than $50,000 toward the cost of legal defense.

We would soon learn that what costs money in lawsuits isn't judgments (we have never had an adverse judgment) but self-defense. The bout referred to here was against a nasty ultra-right hate merchant, ironically represented, in court, by a veteran pro-Communist attorney. On the points in contention the judge found copiously in our favor, but what he awarded us didn't meet one half of one day's legal costs. Well, we are still in business, and I have no doubt that our old insurance company also survives.

It was heartening to receive from the White House a Christmas greeting written in Latin. And we happily recorded that Art Buchwald had gotten a Christmas card from the chairman of Hertz.

Jimmy Carter's speechwriter James Fallows never shared my own enthusiasm for Ronald Reagan, who defeated Carter, notwithstanding the quality of the speeches Fallows crafted for him. Reagan had left the White House by the time Fallows weighed in with some class-warfare talk, ascribing to me pretensions which really didn't fit, though I readily conceded that my grandfather, who was a sheriff in south Texas, had an affinity for Lyndon Johnson: "Although my grandfather died in 1904, he voted for Johnson in 1948."

There was much more—Did I belong in the *Preppy Handbook*? One reader wanted to know whether he dared deposit a check from the U.S. Treasury for $1,000. And there was our surprise, when the end of the line came for the Soviet Union, that it was Gorbachev who had been named the Man of the Decade by *Time* magazine, our candidate being the politician, now retired, who by our reckoning had done the most to close down the Soviet operation. By the end of the period addressed in this chapter, the Soviet Union had dematerialized. I published in the magazine a few paragraphs registering gratitude for the end of the cold war.

February 8, 1980

Dear Bill:

I am surprised that you should fall into the common error that the two men crucified with Jesus Christ were "criminals." True, Josephus called them "brigands" (lestai). But careful Biblical exegesis demonstrates almost conclusively that they were Zealots--members of the Jewish guerrilla movement, religious and political, which fought to drive out the Romans. (It was the Zealots who perished to the last man, woman, and child in the defense of Masada.)

For their "subversive" activities Zealots were frequently crucified by the Romans. There are veiled references to the Zealots, among whom Jesus grew up, in the Gospels--and, in fact, one of the Apostles is designated a Zealot by Mark, who calls him "Simon Kananaois," the Aramaic word for Zealot.

As always,
Ralph [de Toledano]
Washington, D.C.

Memo to: Malachi Martin [NR's religion editor]
From: WFB

Help!

Dear Bill:

The weight of objective evidence supports the translation of "criminals" or "evildoers"--as a general term without specification. Here is the evidence.

In three Gospels, the two crucified with Jesus are described as:

1) κακοῦργος, by Luke, three times (23, 32; 23, 33; 23, 39);

2) λῃστής, by Mark, once (15, 27); by Matthew, twice (27, 38; 27, 44). John refers merely to ἄλλους δύο ("two others"), without further specification.

The word κακοῦργος occurs in the New Testament only four times. Indubitably, it refers always to what we would express by the general term "criminal" or "evildoer." The word λῃστής occurs in the New Testament 15 times. Again and indubitably, it always refers to "criminals" or "evildoers," but with a note of specification--robbery, homicide, cheating. Where either word occurs in the Greek of the Old Testament (the Septuagint) it invariably means the same as when it is used in the New Testament. . . .

So the linguistic argument is irrefragable for opting for "criminals" as a general term. Only, λῃστής is derived from a root conveying the idea of "prey" or "booty." Hence it adds the specification of robbery and homicide. The other word is formed with the root meaning "evil," "harm," "wrong." In all events, the two gentlemen were hard cases.

The idea of treating the two "criminals" as Zealots is not new, but it has received tremendous vogue in the last fifty years because of the efforts to make the execution of Jesus--as well as the nature of his "movement" and "preaching"--appear purely political. Hence He is made to seem merely a Jewish political leader, not a savior. Only He messed up His act, like so many other self-appointed Messiahs (all political) who plagued the Greek and Roman occupations of Judea in the last one hundred years before Jesus. . . . By the way, it is misleading to say that the Zealots "perished to the last man, woman, and child in the defense of Masada." They committed suicide--an important point. They chose

mass suicide, rather than fall into the hands of the
Romans. Hence the talk about the "Masada complex" of
modern Israel--which has now become the "Gaza complex"
(if we go down, we will tear the house down with us).

There have been huge efforts to place Jesus in
the Judea of his time as a revolutionary with a
socio-political program backed up (as always with
ancient Jewish leaders) with a religious program.
And the efforts are part of the "liberation theology"
and what one might call the Che-Guevara-ing of Jesus.
There is no scholarship in all this, merely the
layering over of Jesus' salvific work with a modern
socio-political ideology. And this madness will last
for some time, because faith is weak.

Hope that all this helps. Briefly, stick to your guns.

Best always,
Malachi

Dear Ralph: Put that in your pipe and smoke it! Cordially, Bill

May 2, 1980

February 18, 1980

The Honorable Ronald Reagan
Los Angeles, Calif. 90024

Dear Ron:

You undoubtedly have seen the Haynes Johnson piece in the *Washington Post* for February 4. He made the following statement: "And Reagan can be capable of flat-out misstatements of facts. Thus, in every address last week he said: 'Arriving in Warsaw in 1977 President Carter got off the plane to announce to a startled satrap who rules that country on behalf of the Soviet Union, "Our concept of human rights is preserved in Poland." What concept of human rights can that be? Would he like to explain that to millions of Polish-Americans who know better . . . '

"Carter never said any such thing."

Haynes Johnson is correct, but he might have been a little bit more cautious. Here is what Carter said on arriving in Poland: namely that Poland was a "partner in a common effort against war and deprivation." That was on September 30, 1977.

But on April 12, 1978, toasting Ceausescu of Rumania, Carter announced that "the people of the United States are honored by having as their guest a great leader of a great country. Our goals are also the same, to have a just system of economics and politics, to let the people of the world share in growth, in peace, in personal freedom." So you have to clean up your act a little bit, but not by much. Warm regards.

As ever,
Bill

March 14, 1980

Mr. William F. Buckley Jr.
Editor
National Review

Dear Bill:

Thank you for your letter about the Johnson piece in the *Washington Post*. Now, hoping I won't seem ungrateful, I have an opportunity that I seldom, if ever, have had to add to your store of information.

I guess my principal mistake with regard to the President and his statement in Poland was that I made it sound as if he spoke those words upon arriving and getting off the airplane. Bill, he actually did make that statement, but he made it the next day at a luncheon. Our records show that he again made very much the same statement about our concept of human rights being preserved in Poland on a later occasion on the same visit. By later, I mean within 24 hours of the first statement. Anyway, you were good to take this matter up and provide me with the additional information.

I hope you're having a wonderful time there [in Switzerland] on the ski slopes. If you look up and see something familiar sailing through the air, it is me wafted aloft by the [primary] results in South Carolina, Georgia, Florida, and Alabama. I know I won't have that easy a time in Illinois. Anderson seems to have captured even the *Tribune*.

Now, of course, we anxiously await the word from Mount Olympus as to whether there will be a Ford in my future. As I dictate this, he's in Washington talking to a group of congressmen who, from all I learn, are not at all happy about the prospect of his getting in the race. I hope he'll think it over and realize that what he's proposing and the way he's doing it could be very divisive and, once again, the Republicans would be trying to win a convention rather than an election.

Best regards,
Ron

June 13, 1980

Miss Virginia B. Smith
President
Vassar College
Poughkeepsie, N.Y.

Dear Miss Smith:

On March 20 you sent me a telegram the first sentence of which read, "The Class of 1980 at Vassar College invites you to speak at their graduation on the morning of Sunday, May 25, 1980."

On March 24, acknowledging my acceptance, you began your letter, "I am delighted that you have agreed to be our Commencement speaker. I shall inform the president of the senior class when the students return from spring vacation today, and I know that the class will be pleased and excited."

On April 24, someone from your office called my secretary to ask if I might make a special pre-Commencement appearance at Vassar—to "answer a few questions some of the students have raised." I asked to be informed about the character of those questions. On April 30 I received your letter, beginning with the sentence, "Spring at Vassar is traditionally lively," and enclosing four issues of the Vassar student newspaper, revealing among other things that 53 per cent of the class now opposed the invitation. Having read those issues, on May 2 I telephoned you with a proposal I deemed appropriate. You replied that you thought my idea useful, would consult with your colleagues, and would get back to me on May 6.

However, I did not hear from you again until May 14, when you left word with my office (I was traveling) where I could reach you on May 15. You discussed my proposal, the reasons you now thought it inadvisable, and once again reconfirmed the invitation. I advised you that I would reflect, over the weekend, on the whole matter, and communicate with you on Monday. This I am now doing.

I decline the invitation to participate in Vassar's Commencement exercises.

You stressed the point, in your open letter to the student body of April 21, that you had invited me pursuant to established procedures for selecting a Commencement speaker. I do not doubt that you did, but there is no gainsaying, notwithstanding that your invitation was issued in the name of the senior class, that a numerical majority of that same class have recorded their opposition to my speaking at Commencement.

Moreover, I tend to agree that Commencement speakers are an integral part of the ceremony, broadly viewed; and although Commencement speakers cannot reasonably be expected to incarnate the institution at which they speak (unless they are Douglas MacArthur, addressing West Point), their physical presence should not ordinarily be offensive to the majority of the graduating class: indeed, it is for this reason that most colleges consult the senior class on the matter of a Commencement speaker.

The majority of the senior class of Vassar does not desire my company, and I must confess, having read specimens of their thoughts and sentiments, that I do not desire the company of the majority of the senior class of Vassar. Really, they appear to be a fearfully ill-instructed body, to judge from the dismayingly uninformed opinions expressed in their newspaper, which opinions reflect an academic and cultural training very nearly unique—at least, in my experience. I have spoken, I suppose, at five hundred colleges and universities in the past thirty years, and nowhere have I encountered that blend of ferocious illiteracy achieved by the young men and women of Vassar who say they speak for the majority of the graduating class and, to some extent, say so plausibly by adducing the signatures of the majority of that class in their recall petition. One professor of English writes to the newspaper, "It was Buckley who offered pridefully in those days the caste of mind and insinuating attitudes toward academics which intellectually veneered the crudities of Joe McCarthy, and in so doing, fueled 'McCarthyism' at its most virulent pitch with respect to the academic community." That the man who composed that sentence should be teaching English at Vassar rather than studying it suggests that Vassar has much, much deeper problems than coming up with a suitable Commencement speaker.

I thank you for your kindnesses, and apologize for the inconvenience, for which, however, I think you will agree I am not wholly to blame.

Yours faithfully,
Wm. F. Buckley Jr.

November 14, 1980

Dear Bill:

    You figure most agreeably in Evelyn Waugh's letters, which I am currently reviewing. It was a major act of imagination but contrary to the basic principles

of the free-enterprise system that the younger Buckley
should ask the greatest prosemaster of the century to
write for *National Review* for, I figure, $200 a time.
I believe it is called hard-headed philanthropy.

Out of friendship and a well-known ability to corrupt,
I am concealing your whole relationship with Waugh.

Yours faithfully,
Ken [John Kenneth Galbraith]
Harvard University
Cambridge, Mass.

Dear Ken:

Your mathematics are, for once, counter-inflationary. I figure it came
to slightly over $400 a time, and that was three Democratic
Administrations back, i.e., real money.

Mark Amory, the editor of *The Letters of Evelyn Waugh* (London,
Ticknor & Fields, 1980), did a curiously selective job of presenting
Waugh's letters to me. Certainly (see below) the editor conveyed the
impression that Waugh thought poorly of National Review and—can
you believe it?—of my own writing. I am publishing (marked with an
asterisk: *) the letters reproduced in the collection. I intersperse letters
not reproduced in the collection. These letters, to say the least, suggest
that, on the subject of National Review and my own readability, Mr.
Waugh's views matured. It is, you will agree—will you not?—a pity that
the later Waugh's views were kept from you.

Yours cordially,
Bill

*February 29, 1960, WFB writes to Evelyn Waugh to comment on Waugh's
expressed skepticism in reviewing Richard Rovere's book on McCarthy for the*
Spectator. *WFB offers to send Waugh a copy of Buckley and Bozell's* McCarthy

and His Enemies *(Chicago: Regnery, 1954)*. "Probably you will not want to spend the time necessary to learn the story, which is understandable. But I urge you then to heed the misgivings you clearly feel and give anti-McCarthyism a wide berth in the future." *WFB's P.S.:* "I am sending you a copy of my book *Up from Liberalism*. Please read the chapter on the great anti-McCarthy confidence man, Paul Hughes (p. 70). You will never forget that story."

FROM MR. E. WAUGH, COMBE FLOREY HOUSE, NR. TAUNTON

Many thanks for your interesting letter. If you can spare a copy of your *McCarthy & His Enemies* I should greatly like to read it.

EW
5th March 1960

March 22, 1960, WFB replies that he is dispatching a copy of McCarthy and His Enemies. *"I enclose the current issue of* National Review *because you may want to see Colm Brogan's description of the British hysteria."*

* [published in *The Letters of Evelyn Waugh*]

To WILLIAM F. BUCKLEY   COMBE FLOREY HOUSE

4 April 1960

Dear Mr. Buckley:
  I have to thank you for a) *Up from Liberalism*, b) *McCarthy and His Enemies* and c) the *National Review* containing Colm Brogan's description of "British hysteria." I don't think you must take the last too seriously. McCarthy is certainly regarded by most Englishmen as a regrettable figure and your *McCarthy and His Enemies*, being written before his later extravagances, will not go far to clear his

reputation. I have no doubt that we were sent a lot
of prejudiced information six years ago. Your book
makes plain that there was a need for investigation
ten years ago. It does not, I am afraid, supply the
information that would convince me that McCarthy was
a suitable man to undertake it. Rovere makes a number
of precise charges against his personal honour.
Until these are rebutted those who sympathise with
his cause must deplore his championship of it.

Yours sincerely,
Evelyn Waugh

May 24, WFB acknowledges Waugh's letter, and comments, "For the record, I should like to remind you that the virulence of the anti-McCarthy press was as marked at the time I wrote my book as it is now. . . . Believe me, I am not saying all this because I care so much at this point for historical rectification (I have other things on my mind). But I care that you should not be victimized by the myth-makers. You have not spent your life jumping through their hoops, and you are too venerable to begin." *WFB offers Waugh a subscription to* National Review. "If you champion McCarthy's cause, while deploring his championship of it, you should look, now and then, at *National Review*. We do not make the mistakes he made and, Deo volente, never shall. . . ."

On May 30, 1960, WFB was sent by an old friend a clipping from the Manchester Guardian *reporting on a speech by Waugh in which he complained of the niggardly returns on his biography of Ronald Knox.* ("At this rate, I shall end my life writing a history of the cobbler industry.") *Without alluding to the article, WFB wrote to Waugh on May 31, 1960, asking if he would be interested in writing a monthly letter.* "I am prepared, because of the admiration which I and the editors have for your writing, to offer you a guarantee of $5,000 a year for a piece every few weeks, of two thousand words. That is higher pay by far than we have given before, higher than what we have paid to Max Eastman, John Dos Passos, Whittaker Chambers, and other freelance writers who have frequently written for us . . ."

* To WILLIAM F. BUCKLEY   COMBE FLOREY HOUSE

3 June 1960

Dear Mr. Buckley,

   Thank you for your letter of 31st May.
   It is most gratifying that you would like me to contribute to the *National Review* & I appreciate that in the circumstances your offer is a generous one, but until you get much richer (which I hope will be soon) or I get much poorer (which I fear may be sooner) I am unable to accept it.

Yours truly,
Evelyn Waugh

* To TOM DRIBERG   COMBE FLOREY HOUSE [6 JUNE 1960]

[Postcard]
Dear Tom,

   I read with great interest your article on the new Buchmanism in *New Statesman & Nation*. Can you tell me: did you in your researches come across the name of Wm. F. Buckley Jr., editor of a New York, neo-McCarthy magazine named *National Review*? He has been showing me great & unsought attention lately & your article made me curious. Has he been supernaturally "guided" to bore me? It would explain him.

Yours ever,
Evelyn

11 June 1960

Dear Tom,

. . . I have thrown away all copies of *National Review*.
These are the directors. Only one familiar name, Chambers
(who kept secret documents in a pumpkin). Buckley
wrote *Up from Liberalism* (unreadable); his magazine is
mostly devoted to attacks on American "Liberals." I don't
think he is a Papist. He would have told me, I think,
if he were. Chambers certainly espoused some form of
Christianity--Quaker? It would be interesting to know
if this was a nest of Buchmanites . . .

Yours ever,
Evelyn

*In the spring of 1961, Waugh consented to WFB's request to review Garry Wills's
book on Chesterton* [Chesterton: Man and Mask; *New York: Sheed and Ward,
1961*]. *The review was published in the issue of April 22, 1961.* ("A second
cause which Chesterton might have for complaint is Mr. Wills's literary style.
It is not uniformly bad. Indeed, again and again he shows himself capable of
constructing a grammatical, even an elegant, sentence. . . . [Chesterton] was
a lovable and much loved man abounding in charity and humility. Humility
is not a virtue propitious to the artist. It is often pride, emulation, avarice,
malice—all the odious qualities—which drive a man to complete, elaborate,
refine, destroy, renew, his work until he has made something that gratifies
his pride and envy and greed. And in doing so he enriches the world more
than the generous and good, though he may lose his own soul in the process.
That is the paradox of artistic achievement.")

COMBE FLOREY HOUSE,
COMBE FLOREY,
NR. TAUNTON.

October 27th, 1962

Dear Mr. Buckley,

I have just finished an article of about 3,500 words, which will eventually appear in the English *Spectator*, on the subject of the Vatican Council.

As you know, the Council will sit for a long time before any decisions are made, so there is no urgency about publication. The *Spectator* can delay publication until it appears in America.

The title is "The Same Again Please: An English Layman's Hopes of the Vatican Council." The theme is that the Conciliar Fathers have been imposed on by a minority, comprising an unholy alliance of modernists & archaeologists, into supposing that there is a strong demand among the laity for changes in the liturgy. Hands off the Mass.

I have not yet offered it to any American magazine. Would you care to make an offer for it before I put it into the hands of my agent?

Perhaps you would be so kind as to reply by cable.

Yours sincerely,
Evelyn Waugh

We agreed on a fee, and the essay appeared in the December 4 issue.

COMBE FLOREY HOUSE,
COMBE FLOREY,
NR. TAUNTON.

2nd April 63

Dear Mr. Buckley,

Very many thanks for *Rumbles*. [*Rumbles Left and Right*, by WFB, New York: Putnam's, 1962.]

Some of the essays were familiar to me from *National Review*. I reread them with the same zest as those which were new. You have the very rare gift of captivating the reader's attention in controversies in which he has no direct concern. I congratulate you on the collection. At your best you remind me of Belloc; at your second best of Randolph Churchill.

I hope you enjoyed your visit to London. I never go there nowadays except on my way somewhere else. They have destroyed all its character both architecturally and socially.

Please accept my greetings for Easter (which I shall be spending in Rome).

Yours sincerely,
Evelyn Waugh

March 6, 1981

Dear Bill:

On arriving home I found your novel *Who's on First* and read it immediately. I found it most exciting. But I clearly see the difficulty German publishers have with your novels. You should know that we do not have thrillers in German. We don't even have a word for it. (Only one or two books by Helen MacInnes have been translated and no one ever heard of them.) Detective

stories are something else, because there you have a
riddle, which the reader is challenged to solve.

But when your book appears in German, you should make
some corrections, or run the risk that pedantic
readers will pick them up. Germans are sticklers!

pp. 2-5: Dohany Street in Budapest is in the heart of
the shabby Jewish district, but Pest, unlike Buda, is
a *very* recent city. No Gothic houses, no cobblestones.

p. 5: Not impossible, but most unlikely that a
Hungarian girl should be called "Frieda." Call her
Maria, Sarolta, Kinga, or Judit (Juci), or Etelka,
Dohány is better than Dohany. People might remember
Dohenny!!! Incidentally, Dohány means tobacco and you
mention Tobacco Road.

p. 30: Pokrovskiy is more likely than Pekrovskii.

p. 34: Stick to one transliteration: Vitkovsky. The
right ending of these Russian names is, in German, "ij":
Witkowskij.

p. 35: Kapitsa is almost impossible since there
exists a famous Russian atomic physicist with the name
of Pyotr Kapitsa--who was kidnapped by the Soviets. If
he hasn't died, he is still alive in the USSR. This is
like inventing an Austrian composer named Kenneth van
Beethoven. Kapitsa is a *very* rare name!

p. 42: Ust' alone is too little. All Ust's in Russia
are hyphenated places. And is there such an Ust' near
Vorkuta? I doubt it.

p. 62: Is that French text faulty on purpose? I think
that it should be correct.

p. 67: Sverdlov did not give the order to execute the
Czar. He carried out the orders of Lenin and Yurkovskiy.

p. 85: Surely Jozsef Nagy? Nadi is *impossible*. Nagy
is OK because it is a very frequent name, like Smith,
or Fisher.

p. 86: Ernö, not Erno.

p. 86: Zlaty is a very un-Hungarian name. (It is Czech.)

IMPORTANT. The Hungarian Revolution of 1956 was *totally* unprepared. It emanated from public meetings of a poetical association.

p. 93: In 1956 a Hungarian beer would not have been obtainable in Paris.

p. 94: Tóth is better than Toth.

p. 125: There is a Ferenc Boulevard or a Ferenc Square, but no Ferenc Street in Budapest.

p. 145: In 1957 a ship going from Odessa to Indonesia would necessarily pass by Bizerta, because the Suez Canal was then closed!!!

p. 149: Louis XIV never said *"L'Etat, c'est moi"*--it is apocryphal. The old czars called themselves *samodyerzhets*, or *avtokrator*, but this term was intended to suggest that they were independent of the Tartars, not that they were absolute monarchs. (There *is* also a Slavic term.)

p. 209: I would transliterate Mechta into Metshtá for the German.

p. 250: It's Punta Delgado.

p. 251: There is no "college" in Sweden--and, I suppose, hardly a single secondary school--teaching Russian.

I am not too happy about the names Spektorsky and Vlasov. The talks between Allen Dulles and Dean Acheson will hardly ring a bell in Germany. Few people realize how stupid Eisenhower was. And how can anybody translate Punky's speech? There are practically no swear words in German. "Kiss my arse" is the only indelicate expression. It is, of course, quite legitimate to introduce real persons. I feel very honored to appear in these pages. One more thing: I have never met a Hungarian with the name of Theophilus. Should be: Teofil.

All the best,
Erik [von Kuehnelt-Leddihn]
Lans, Tyrol, Austria

PS: Ilyitch is a patronymic, not a family name.

PPS: p. 99: The Transsiberian does not run through that area.

   Somewhere in the book, a Russian refers to the "Eastern front." No Russian would have done that, because for him it was a Western front. I don't think that he would have said "the Western front" either, but just: "the Front" (there was an Eastern front for a few days in Eastern Siberia: Manchuria).

   p. 239: No Russian soldier says to a higher officer, "sir." Such a word does not exist in the Soviet language, and I do not even know how a soldier addressed his superior in the Imperial Army. In Germany and Austria it was "Herr Lieutenant," "Herr Major," etc. "Sir" has no Continental equivalent. And "sir" in the USSR is out of the question. In Imperial Russia, in civilian life, *barin* or *gosudar'*.

As ever,
Erik

Dear Erik: Forget it. Am resigning, going back to school. What can I pay you not to read my next book? Gratefully, Bill

August 21, 1981

Dear Mr. Buckley:

   Hello! I am running for the President of the U.S.A. I would like your friendship and help. Bye.

Yours,
Louis Ramsey
Chicago, Ill.

Dear Mr. Ramsey: Hello! I urge you to enter all the Democratic primaries. You are manifestly better qualified than the most conspicuous contenders. Bye. Cordially, WFB

September 18, 1981

Sir:

1. You look sloppy, your shirt needs washing and pressing.
2. Take your hand away from your face!
3. Try to speak clearly--you mumble!
4. Your program is badly run--ill prepared. Try to improve, which might be difficult for you.

Mike McNeil
New York, N.Y.

Dear Mr. McNeil: For me to improve would be not only difficult, but impossible. Cordially, WFB

February 19, 1982

Dear Mr. Buckley:

A bespectacled curator demonstrated Edison's first gramophone. Hairy ironmongers jumped; kindly ladies muttered; nine old parsons quickly retreated, stealthily tiptoeing. "Undoubtedly violins with xylophones," yelled Zeke.

The passage above, as you may have noticed, contains 26 words, the initial letters of which are in alphabetical order, from A to Z. There's a theory (surely there must be) that something of a person's subconscious mind can be discerned by having him (or her) compose such a passage within a period of not more than, oh, twenty minutes, and without the aid

of reference material. Even if there isn't anything
psychoanalytically useful in this little exercise,
I have found it to be an enjoyable and rather
challenging way to spend idle moments.
   Now, the point of my letter, Mr. Buckley. Will you,
when you have the time, please have a go at
constructing an A-through-Z passage of your own? And
if you will, and if you don't mind the inconvenience,
will you then mail the result to me? I'd be grateful.

Quite sincerely,
John Luker
Kingston, Ont.

*Dear Mr. Luker: Alphabet? Bright chap demonstrated . . . Eek! forgoshsakes,
g h i j k l m n o p q r s t u v w x, you zombie. —WFB*

April 2, 1982

Dear Mr. Buckley:

   Alphabetical fascination does not afflict Mr. Luker
alone. Alas, I too am infected. Hence, a tribute:
   Academician Buckley countered Democratic expletives,
feuding graciously, hilariously immolating jargon-
knitting liberal magniloquence. "No obfuscation?"
piquantly queried *Review*. "Stultifying trendiness!
Undiscriminating volubility will X yammering zealots."

Sincerely,
Christina L. Rizzo
Baltimore, Md.

Miss Rizzo: Nice going. —WFB

July 23, 1982

Mr. Mark Amory
Ticknor & Fields
London

Dear Mr. Amory:

I'm not sure why I put off writing to you for so long. Perhaps it was my general admiration for the job you did in editing the letters of Mr. Evelyn Waugh [*The Letters of Evelyn Waugh*, edited by Mark Amory, New Haven: Ticknor & Fields, 1980].

But now, with yet another smirking allusion in the press—this one by Herb Caen, in the *San Francisco Chronicle*—to the low opinion Waugh had of me, my magazine, and my abilities, I must ask you for an explanation.

1. I enclose a copy of the column by Mr. Caen. I enclose a copy of the letter that I addressed to Mr. Caen.

2. I enclose a copy of the feature "Notes & Asides" from *National Review*, November 14, 1980. I should have addressed a copy of that feature to you at the time, so that I'd have had access to your explanation for the missing letters, EW to WFB.

3. My confusion is reinforced by the acknowledgments in your book. Apparently I gave you permission to enter my files and to take from them copies of letters from EW to me. When the book came out, I asked the Yale University Library, which keeps my papers, to give me in turn copies of letters from EW to WFB. I instantly received the entire set published in the *National Review* feature. It is, I should think, logical to conclude that you were in possession of the identical set. Why then did you not, even if you elected not to publish any of his subsequent letters to me, mention in a footnote that Mr. Waugh was friendly to me, and to my journal? I am most anxious for your explanation, as it will facilitate my handling of my critics, who are greatly enjoying themselves on this point.

I am sending a copy of this letter and enclosures to Auberon Waugh, not in the spirit of intimidation but because, as an old personal friend, I would not want him to be surprised that there was contention, so to speak, in the family.

Yours faithfully,
Wm. F. Buckley Jr.

COMBE FLOREY HOUSE

SOMERSET, ENGLAND

Dear Bill:

Thank you for sending me your correspondence with Mark Amory. I am sorry that he seems to be making cheap capital from the few rude references to you in my Father's correspondence. If he had known you better there would probably have been more of them, but that would not mean that he held you in anything but greatest esteem. He always spoke of you with admiration, as I remember, and was delighted when I started writing for you many years ago.

The problem with opening anyone's letters or diaries is that one is bound to find unkind references to friends, relations, and even strangers which the writer would never have intended to see published. It was a difficulty which I met, particularly in the Diaries, by a blanket policy of publishing everything. There were many extraordinarily rude references to myself and other members of the family, both in the Diaries and in the Letters. My policy was to hide nothing simply on the grounds that it would have been rather a despicable thing to discriminate. We all write unkind jokes and even deeply wounding remarks about our best friends in circumstances where we do

not expect them to read them. One just has to learn not
to take offense. But I am sorry that people are using
these references to embarrass you. The only policy in
my experience is to rise above it all. One of the joys
of journalism is that everybody forgets it within a
week or two.

Mark Amory is a very old friend of mine, but of course
he is a Liberal. His mother decided to stand as Liberal
candidate while he was at Oxford, and the result is to
be found in a little-read novel of mine called *Path of
Dalliance*, where she appears as Mrs. Sligger. I am
sure that no malice is intended, merely the impulsive
journalistic urge to make jokes.

Have you ever been to Combe Florey? I hope we may
tempt you down here one day. I practically never leave
nowadays except for twice-yearly pilgrimages to the
Far East, but it would be lovely to see you again,
when you are in England. I was in Cuba two weeks ago
and brooded on the terrible struggle in your breast
between patriotism and appreciation of good cigars
which you somehow resolved by leaving a box of Cuban
cigars in my house in Wiltshire. There is a fast train
service from London if ever you are tempted.

All the best.

Yours ever,
Bron
[Auberon Waugh]

Dear Mr. Buckley:

When I asked for letters from Evelyn Waugh, I was
indeed sent the complete set and I am sorry to have
returned evil for good. I edited ruthlessly on grounds
of interest or amusement, fairness coming a poor

third. Certainly your relationship with Waugh was
distorted as a result. His rudeness about you was
clearly meant to cheer up Driberg, an old friend whose
book you had criticized. My explanation will not seem
strong to you but was for me: to put in corrective
footnotes throughout would have been laborious, dull
to read, and lead into the tricky, almost impossible,
area of deciding how much of what Waugh said he meant.

   You have my sympathy and my apologies for the
resulting annoyance but I see that they are not much
good to you.

Yours sincerely,
Mark Amory

Dear Auberon:

   *I attach this note to my letter [not here reproduced] to you, as I have just
seen Mark Amory's letter, a copy of which I enclose. I have decided it doesn't
require an answer.*

   As ever,
   Bill

August 20, 1982

Miss Mary McGrory
Washington Post
Washington, D.C.

Dear Mary:

   I note your words, "He [Reagan] gave no indication of how he did his
research. Did Claudette Colbert, his hostess, fill him in? Or was it his
fellow guest, the millionaire columnist William F. Buckley Jr.?" I write to

ask whether your assumption is that millionaire columnists are not capable of doing research.

If so, is there a McGrory Corollary, to the effect that the validity of research is in inverse proportion to the wealth of the researcher? If so, would it be as fair for me in writing about you, as it was presumably fair for you in writing about me, to make the same assumption? Should I ask that you append to any column of yours that required research some indication of your economic circumstances? Can we assume that Bill Moyers's research is tainted by his income, which I would gladly trade my own income for? Or do we simply assume that Dear Mary can't think either straight or honorably when she deals with human misery? And speaking of corollaries, should we assume that medical surgeons who do not weep for the plight of their patients while practicing their profession are hard of heart?

I'd ever so much appreciate an elucidation.

As ever,
Bill

September 3, 1982

Dear Mr. Buckley:

I do not wish to be a pedant, but I really must object to an item in the June 25 issue of *NR*. I hope I beat Erik von Kuehnelt-Leddihn to the punch on this one. On page 739 you make a joking reference to Yuri Andropov, identifying him as "Tsarytsyn, or heir apparent." The Russian word for heir apparent, problems of transliteration aside, is "tsarevich," and is not capitalized. "Tsarytsyn" is an old form of the possessive. To be sure, both of these words mean, roughly, "son of the tsar." The usages are, however, entirely different.

"Tsarytsyn" would do for a last name, or even for a place name (see pre-revolutionary Stalingrad, for example). "Tsarevich" is exclusively the title of the heir apparent.

I appreciate the jest. Still, I find it hard to believe that you do not have anyone on your staff who speaks Russian. Come now, Mr. Buckley, you know how important it is to know your enemy.

Yours in Freedom,
Barry A. Zulauf
Political Science
Indiana University
Bloomington, Ind.

Dear Professor Zulauf: When the Russians come, we don't intend to speak to them, in any language. Cordially, WFB

Dear Mr. Buckley:

If a liberal calls me a Fascist because I am a conservative, what should I do? Should I:
  a) diplomatically ignore the hyperbole;
  b) say: "When I become dictator, you'll go into the camps!"; or
  c) duke him/her out?

I'm inclined toward c), but, being a Midwesterner, I am oblivious to such matters of etiquette. What is the proper response? Any suggestions would be appreciated greatly.

Yours semi-sincerely,
Jeff Tutt
Michigan City, Ind.

Dear Mr. Tutt: You might try, "That's what all the Communists say about me." Granted, that sort of thing is tu quoque. But fascists are famous for that. Cordially, WFB

September 17, 1982

Dear Mr. Buckley:

Boy, do you have a nerve!
After watching the debate on the Reagan budget priorities on *Firing Line*, I wrote away to that incipient fascist dictatorship, otherwise known as South Carolina, for a transcript of Part Two, in which Mr. Oakes nailed you right-wing intellectual poseurs but good. I enclosed a personal check for $2. I put it in the envelope: I distinctly remember I did *not* leave it on the dresser.
Instead of sending me the transcript, months later, you use my name and mailing address to solicit a subscription to your monthly rag. Do you really think I want to waste my time reading about how leading Catholics swear by the morality of the neutron bomb? Over your house, they should detonate it!
Go look up chutzpah in the dictionary.

Sincerely yours,
Harvard Hollenberg
(Associate Counsel)
The Assembly
State of New York
Albany, N.Y.

Dear Mr. Hollenberg: 1) We do not publish a monthly rag, we publish a fortnightly rag. 2) Wasting your time is obviously an imperative social obligation. 3) If a neutron bomb were detonated over my house, my house would survive; which is the point, ass. 4) How else would you expect the incipient fascist dictatorship in South Carolina to act? Cordially, WFB

November 12, 1982

Miss Priscilla Buckley
Managing Editor
National Review

Dear Priscilla:

I'm dying for word on what you thought of my article,
"Going Courting in Washington." But then, I can
imagine the scenario. You'll send it up to Bill in
the dumbwaiter. He'll carry it around for several
weeks unaware that he has it in one of his stuffed
briefcases. Months will pass, after which time,
you'll ask in a note what he thought of it. "Of what?"
he'll ask. You'll explain and he'll swear that he
never saw it. He'll be right. It will have been left
in a hotel room in China. An officious Chinese will
have forwarded it to New York, by which time Bill will
be somewhere in the middle of the Atlantic. A kindly
Coast Guard cutter will pull alongside to deliver the
missing briefcase, but just as the captain is reaching
across the bow the catches on the case will pop open
and my manuscript will float lazily out to sea.

If you need me, I'll be in my room with a hot-water
bottle on my head.

Lots of love,
Mona [Charen]
George Washington Law School
Washington, D.C.

Priscilla: I'll publish this libelous letter. Mona's article is, as you know now,
scheduled. —Bill

```
Memo to: WFB
From: Frances
```

People magazine published your letter in their
current [September 27] issue. The bracketed material
in your original was left out:

Dear Sirs:

[In his column,] "Chatter" [, for September 6, your writer Josh
Hammer] reports that St. John (New Brunswick) businessman Aubrey
Pope caught me, my son, and Professor Thomas Wendel, while cruising
down the St. John River, in flagrante. ". . . three of Buckley's crew
members had indeed sought to unload their trash by dumping it all on
Pope's private dock. Pope happened to intercept them and ordered them
off. 'I'm not very big, but I can get ugly,' he said, adding that he 'would
have been glad to help' if it hadn't been for their 'arrogant attitude.'
Buckley's response was to dump his trash without permission at a scenic
spot farther downriver . . ."

Well, now. 1) Pope didn't "intercept" us. He arrived at his dock as we
arrived at it. 2) We didn't unload the garbage from our dinghy, we asked
whether we might do so, to which his answer was a curt No. 3) We didn't
proceed to dump the trash anywhere, retaining it on board the dinghy
until reaching the Yacht Club the next day. 4) If we had been unconcerned
about pollution, we would quite simply have dumped it into the river in
the first place. I, my son, and Tom Wendel happen, coincidentally, to be
the three politest men alive, and the most responsible. It would not occur
to us to dump garbage on private property without permission [, or to
publish a story to the effect that Mr. Hammer had done so, without first
calling him up and asking him whether so bizarre an allegation by a
small, ugly—and scurrilous—old man was correct].

Yours truly,
Wm. F. Buckley Jr.

December 10, 1982

Dear Bill:

I don't know if you received a similar letter, but we can now earn points for renting Hertz cars. You will note in their last letter that I have been credited fifty bonus points for just being a charter member. I suggest that we each keep the other informed as to how many points we have, and then, on September 30, 1983, we can both take our families to a Marriott hotel in Flint, Michigan.

I feel this Hertz Five Star membership is the thing that binds our friendship, and if it weren't for them we would just be two columnists working different sides of the political fence.

I am calling this point system to your attention on the off chance that your secretary may have thrown your letter in the trash can. Secretaries tend to ignore club news.

Sincerely,
Art [Buchwald]
Washington, D.C.

Dear Art: You ask how many bonus points have I been credited with by Hertz? Art, who won the election in 1980, the Republican, or the Democrat? If it is true that we are working different sides of the political fence, how many points would you give, if you were Hertz, to the columnist who delivered 44 states, as opposed to the columnist who could only limp in with six states? I don't want to advertise, Art, that this is a tough world that apportions perquisites with some consideration of merit, but if you . . . No, with that aposiopesis I change the subject. Let us agree only that we will keep each other informed on how many points we earn beginning at this juncture. My belief in full disclosure impels me to confess that, as I write, my wife is going round and round on the Hawthorne Circle in a Hertz car listening on the cassette player to tapes of your columns, and laughing and laughing, oh my, how she is laughing. Cordially, Bill

January 1, 1983

Dear Mr. Buckley:

   Re: "Notes & Asides," Sept. 17, 1982: A neutron bomb detonated directly over your house would most assuredly demolish it. The "enhanced radiation warhead," while having less of its energy released as blast effect than an atomic bomb (40 per cent instead of 50 per cent), is actually a small hydrogen bomb, with one hundred times the explosive power of the weapons used in World War II.

   Without questioning the desirability of deploying this weapon to defend against a Soviet armored invasion of Europe, I would suggest that you be more precise about your physics, lest you yourself appear to be what you called your critic.

Respectfully yours,
Jane M. Orient, MD
Tucson, Ariz.

Dear Dr. Orient: I meant, explode one hundred miles over my house. If it comes too close, can I call you? Cordially, WFB

December 9, 1983

Dear Mr. Buckley:

"If it feels good, do it" sounds ignoble even when elegantly expressed by Mr. Barzun.

Sincerely,
Laurel Suomisto
Los Angeles, Calif.

Dear Miss Suomisto: Doesn't that depend on what you do to whom? Cordially, WFB

January 27, 1984

Dear Mr. Buckley:

In the current edition of *Time* magazine, you are quoted (in response to the rumor that Paul Newman will narrate a sixty-second spot offering a nuclear-war-prevention kit) as saying, "I plan to write in for one of those kits, and if Mr. Newman doesn't send me an MX missile, I'm going to report him to the Postal Service people for fraud."

I have read that rather remarkable statement several times. I still haven't reached a conclusion. Were you sarcastic, or were you serious? (I find the latter option incomprehensible, but I have learned never to underestimate the opposition, especially if I tend to find them fanatic; one definition of fanatic, as you know, is "intense, uncritical devotion.")

If, by any possible stretch of the imagination, you meant this remark seriously, albeit with a touch of tongue-in-cheek (this is not a conflicting description; think about it), then your attitude is criminal at worst, unconscionable at best.

If it is sarcastic, it is merely irresponsible. In either case it is dangerous.

The only possible nuclear-war-prevention kit would consist of the prayers, pleas, hopes, dreams, and fears of the American people.

Your attitude, no matter what its foundation, reminds me rather uncomfortably of an NRA [National Rifle Association] bumper sticker I saw on the back of (what else?) a pickup truck: "My wife yes, my dog maybe, my gun never."

We are now, unfortunately, living in a kakistocracy. Even more unfortunately, people such as yourself apparently wish this to continue. If we continue to live at all.

Sincerely,
Carly Mary Cady
Los Angeles, Calif.

Dear Miss Cady: But I am entirely serious. I would like my own personal MX missile, even though it would slow me up a little in getting around. Moreover, I would train it on Red Square. Moreover, I would instruct it to fire on warning. I would then extend to all the subscribers to National Review *the immunities of my personal umbrella. You can come too and repent, though in fact you would not need to, exactly for the same reasons that have guided the so-called kakistocracy that has kept you alive, and free, even to write letters consuming the time of those busy looking after your welfare. Cordially, WFB*

June 29, 1984

Dear Bill:

You may be interested in the following exchange.

Best regards,
Chuck [Charlton Heston]
Beverly Hills, Calif.

SENT BY CERTIFIED MAIL
Mr. Charlton Heston
c/o David Capell & Co.
315 South Beverly Drive
Beverly Hills, Calif. 90212

Dear Mr. Heston:

It has come to the attention of the Screen Actors Guild that you appeared in a television commercial for *National Review* magazine. However, our records do not indicate that employment in this TV commercial was covered by a Screen Actors Guild bargaining agreement.

Please be advised that Rule 1 of the Screen Actors Guild Constitution and By-Laws states:

"No member shall work as an actor or make an agreement to work as an actor for any producer who has not executed a basic minimum agreement with the Guild which is in full force and effect."

Based on the above information, it appears that you are in violation of Rule 1. The SAG Board of Directors has asked me to investigate this matter before proceeding with possible disciplinary action pursuant to the Constitution and By-Laws. Kindly complete and return the enclosed questionnaire within the next ten (10) days in order to facilitate this investigation.

Thank you for your cooperation.

Sincerely,
Clinta M. Dayton
Assistant National Executive Secretary
Screen Actors Guild

Dear Miss Dayton:

I have your letter of May 3 advising me that I am in apparent violation of SAG Rule 1 as a result of my appearance in *National Review*'s TV commercial. I have enclosed the Rule 1 inquiry you attached, filled out as instructed.

Since I contributed my services to *National Review* without contract or compensation, I presume the question of SAG jurisdiction is irrelevant. Should this not be the case, I'm afraid I've been in violation of Rule 1 for most of the 34 years I've belonged to the Guild. During that time, I've appeared in literally hundreds of commercials on behalf of scores of organizations, ad hoc groups, and committees, all without compensation. I'm afraid my records are incomplete, but they include the Red Cross, the Cancer Fund, the National Arthritis Foundation, the Mental Health Association, the Braille Institute, the Salvation Army, the Boy Scouts, the Disabled Veterans of America, Northwestern University, UCLA, the United States Army, Navy, and Air Force, the Department of Agriculture, the State of Illinois, a wide spectrum of arts, medical, and environmental groups, as well as candidates for public office from both the Democratic and Republican Parties. If these appearances violate Rule 1, I'm at a loss to understand why my Guild has not previously called this to my attention.

Since your prime concern seems to be with the *NR* commercial, you may well be instituting Rule 1 inquiries on my fellow SAG members Tom Selleck and Ronald Reagan, who also appeared in the commercial. I can attest that they, too, performed without compensation. I hope this simplifies your endeavors and, in my own case, satisfies our Board.

Fraternally,
Charlton Heston

P.S.: It occurs to me that William F. Buckley, the editor of *National Review*, promised to send me some peanut butter in return for my appearance on behalf of his magazine. His commitment was never contractually ratified, nor has it so far been fulfilled. If he does send me the peanut butter, should I return it to stay out of trouble with my Guild?

cc: Ronald Reagan
    Tom Selleck

Dear Chuck: Hang in there, or we will hang together! Regards, Bill

July 27, 1984

Dear Mr. Buckley:

  Here are the results of our poll about your ideas: Do you agree with William F. Buckley? Yes: 76 per cent. No: 15 per cent. No opinion: 9 per cent. That's very nice. Congratulations.

Cordially yours,
Mihai Dediu
President, Dediu Consulting Institute
Lakewood, Ohio

Dear Dr. Dediu: Your consulting institute is obviously successful three-quarters of the time. Congratulations, WFB

August 24, 1984

Dear Bill:

  I don't like to brag, but I have just received a PLATINUM card from Hertz. There is nowhere you can go after platinum except possibly plutonium.
  I'm really afraid to carry the card in my pocket because in case of a stickup it would be the first one the

thieves would go for. Rumor has it that the underworld will now kill for a Platinum card. You and I have both come a long way in the journalism profession, but I don't know how much higher you can go in life than to become the owner of a Hertz Platinum card. I would say we have achieved the American Dream.

Sincerely,
Art [Buchwald]
Washington, D.C.

Dear Art: The only reason you got a Platinum Hertz card, and I know this for a fact, is that you tipped off the company it would be Geraldine [Ferraro] in San Francisco. Well, I've just tipped them off that Geraldine will be a has-been after November. I expect my card in the next mail. Cordially, Bill

October 5, 1984

Dear Mr. Buckley:

I thought you might be interested in the enclosed correspondence regarding our *National Review* commercial.

I think the Screen Actors Guild's "investigation" into this matter clearly demonstrates their continuing politicization. In their fervor to punish and thus correct this impure thinking, they totally disregarded the fact that they have no jurisdiction in the matter, whatsoever.

The American Federation of Television and Radio Artists' subsequent insistence on my receiving payment for the commercial is even more insidious because it seeks to prohibit me from freely giving that which is my own; namely my time and labor. This is wrong!

I have returned the payment to you and am looking into my legal remedies in the matter. If you need my services

for "The Return of the *National Review* Commercial,"
I will be pleased and honored to donate them.

Sincerely,
Tom Selleck
Honolulu, Hawaii

Miss Clinta M. Dayton
Screen Actors Guild

Re: Tom Selleck/*National Review* magazine commercial

Dear Miss Dayton:

We represent Tom Selleck with regard to various
legal matters. Reference is made to your letter to
Mr. Selleck, dated May 3, 1984, in which you stated,
on behalf of the Screen Actors Guild, that there
appeared to be a violation by Mr. Selleck of Rule 1 of
the SAG Constitution and By-Laws and that the SAG Board
of Directors had asked you to "investigate" this matter
before proceeding with possible disciplinary action
pursuant to the SAG Constitution and By-Laws.

After SAG was informed by Bettye McCartt,
Mr. Selleck's agent, that the commercial was done
under AFTRA jurisdiction for National Media Group
and R. M. Marketing, you acknowledged in your letter
dated May 7, 1984, that "no SAG Rule 1 violation
occurred and therefore no disciplinary action is
warranted," since the employment occurred within the
jurisdiction of AFTRA for an AFTRA signatory.

Mr. Selleck is justifiably shocked and distressed
that the Screen Actors Guild, of which he has been a
member for 17 years, would pursue this reckless,
irresponsible, and vindictive course of action against
him, particularly where SAG did not even have any
jurisdiction regarding the matter and did not make any

inquiry concerning the basis for its jurisdiction and accusations, and apparently asserted the accusations for improper purposes.

. . . This type of coercive intimidation is reminiscent of the insidious way in which fundamental freedoms are lost or subjugated, particularly where the action is taken in the purported name of some other principle such as the enforcement of Guild rules. The chilling effect of this cannot be ignored, and should not be tolerated.

On Mr. Selleck's behalf, we would like to register our strong protest concerning SAG's handling of this matter, and we would request that there be some explanation as to why the Guild took this action, why the Guild made no threshold inquiry concerning its jurisdiction before making irresponsible accusations, and whether SAG communicated with AFTRA regarding this matter.

Sincerely,
John H. Lavely Jr.
Lavely & Singer
Los Angeles, Calif.

Dear Mr. Selleck: Attaboy! Congratulations and, yet again, thanks. —WFB

October 19, 1984

Dear Mr. Buckley:

Your portrait on the jacket of *Up from Liberalism* looks more like Walter Mondale than does Walter Mondale. Perhaps you should have a Secret Service guard.

Sincerely,
Richard W. Whyte
Vienna, Va.

Dear Mr. Whyte: Perhaps I should have an exorcist! Cordially, WFB

November 16, 1984

Dear Mr. Buckley:

I enjoyed the feature on light-bulb humor ["The Gentleman's Light-Bulb Jokes," Sept. 21]. But Mr. Grove's selection omitted what I have always considered the classic of the genre:

Q: How many liberals does it take to change a light bulb?

A: Six; one to screw it in, and five to write the environmental-impact statement.

Sincerely,
Arthur L. Smith
Annandale, Va.

December 28, 1984

THE WHITE HOUSE
WASHINGTON, D.C.

Dear Bill:

Diem natalis felicem vobis desidero et uterque multos annos prospiciamus.

Nancy joins me in these sentiments and we pray that God will bless and keep you.

Sincerely,
Ronald Reagan

Dear Mr. President: Fiat voluntas tua. Ever, Bill

Dear Bill:

Mr. Arthur L. Smith has it wrong ["Notes & Asides," Nov. 16]. The answer to the question, How many liberals

does it take to change a light bulb? is not: Six; one to
screw it in, and five to write the environmental-impact
statement. Rather, it is: Six; five to screw it in, and
one to screw it up.

Affectionately,
Reid [F. R. Buckley]*

April 5, 1985

Dear WFB:

It is my understanding that dissenter Janeski
Fondavich, prima ballerina, has been rewarded for her
performance in the Afghan countryside by being
furnished an all-expenses-paid five-year visit to a
modern medical facility in the Ural Mountains region
of Siberia. Why aren't we as generous with our artists?

Sincerely,
Gerald J. Urpschot
New Orleans, La.

*Dear Mr. Urpschot: Because the Reagan Administration is lacking in
compassion and in an appreciation of the arts. Yours cordially, WFB*

May 31, 1985

Dear Bill:

I've been a subscriber and a sometime contributor
to *NR* for many years because I like its style and, in

---

*My brother Reid is the founder and head of the acclaimed Buckley School of Public
Speaking in Camden, S.C.

general, its philosophy. I must tell you that I am not all that interested in Catholic activities to the extent that you present them. Indeed, you dwell on them as though *NR* were written solely for a Catholic audience. It's boring.

Very truly yours,
Earl Hazan
Barrington, R.I.

Dear Mr. Hazan: If you have especially in mind the space NR *has devoted to the abortion issue,* NR *replies by saying that the issue is falsely identified as a "Catholic" issue. The question whether life exists prebirth is a biological question with moral implications. If you have in mind the coverage given to the increasing politicization of religion by many prominent Catholics, then your own focus, if religion or Catholicism bores you, should be on the politics of the question, not the religion. If you have in mind our general coverage of religion, pray remember that our first religion editor was a Jew (Will Herberg), whose successor was an Anglican (Gerhart Niemeyer), followed by an ex-priest (Malachi Martin), and now—a Catholic (Michael Novak). The editors continue to believe that religion is a part of the historical narrative we seek to chronicle, analyze, and affect. Yours cordially, WFB*

July 12, 1985

Dear Mr. Buckley:

I have invented a new verb: Buckley.
Definition: To dress up a falsehood with eloquent language, with the result that it appears to be true. Thus, if Conservative A and Conservative B are discussing plans to publish a falsehood, Conservative A might say: "Wait a minute. We can't print that in its present form: it's clearly and obviously false." Then

Conservative B could say: "Don't worry. We'll Buckley it: Then it'll appear to be true. Then whoever reads it will believe it." Then Conservative A could say: "Oh. Good idea. Wonderful."

Cordially,
Hank Green
Denver, Colo.

Dear Mr. Green: You have it almost right. What's missing is only that if it is Buckleyed, it not only appears correct, it becomes correct. So you get a B plus. Cordially, WFB

July 26, 1985

Dear Mr. Buckley:

In your review of *The Tenth Man* in *The New York Times Book Review*, you wrote: "And early on in the book . . ." I've come to expect from you a certain care with the language. I don't understand this usage. I've noticed its regular occurrence lately and assumed it was incorrectly modeled on "later on," and was just another of the linguistic fads which come and go like pop songs. I thought Howard Cosell was responsible for it. Like him, it seems redundant.

I don't mean to be a noodge. I understand that mixing levels of usage can be part of style. I can live with "OK" and "guy" for that reason. But please explain why a man who respects infinitives (correctly) would feel comfortable with "early on in."

Sincerely,
Richard Hill
Linville Falls, N.C.

Dear Mr. Hill: A couple of things. First, you cheated a little by asking whether I really liked the sound of "early on in," which sounds awful but entirely begs the question whether "early on" is legitimately used. The "in" would need to be there irrespective of whether the "on" was there. The "on" is neither legitimized nor illegitimized by the ensuing "in"—you with me, Mr. Hill? . . . Anyway, as you know, American idiom tends to add the redundant preposition; thus Americans will often "lift it up off the table," and "enter into the fray." There is a sense in which, by using the preposition, you induce a sense of languor, desirable in the situation described in the book review from which you quote. "Early in life, John showed an interest in Shakespeare" tells you something just a little different from "Early on in life, John showed an interest . . ." A little overtone of precocity in the latter, missing from the former: and a sense of easing into Shakespeare from the cradle, rather than discovering Shakespeare one fine day as, one fine day, I discovered Red Wing Peanut Butter. Enough? Cordially, WFB

October 4, 1985

Dear Mr. Buckley:

1. By any reasonable definition of "redundant," a word in a given context cannot be both a) productive of a desired expressive increment and b) redundant. You demonstrated such valuable increment for your use of "on" in a particular occurrence of "early on"; therefore you had no need to defend it against a charge of redundancy.

2. The expression "early on" is originally British idiom (first *Oxford English Dictionary* citation: Dorothy Sayers, 1928), though by now, obviously, we Americans are in the process of making it American idiom.

3. Besides "early on," your two additional examples of what you call the redundancy of American idiom,

"enter into the fray" and "lift it up off the table,"
are neither inherently redundant (you've given no
context) nor characteristically American (see the
unabridged *OED*). To consider the first example: To enter
the fray suggests a man politely walking through a
gate or, in another context, signals laconism; to
enter into the fray conveys a sense of violent
movement, intrusion, or even a becoming incorporated
with the object. No doubt an undiscriminating user of
the language would regard these two expressions as
interchangeable. Would you define American idiom, or
any nation's idiom, by that exemplar, its least
discriminating user? Do you accord the same
ontological niche to, let us say, Martha Graham and
Dallas?

   4. Only last week a reviewer in the *Times Literary
Supplement* (July 19, B. A. Farrell) took a book
to task for the not-otherwise-specified deficiency of
being "written in American idiom." Happily, you've
cited yourself as an exemplar of American idiom so
that I can infer American idiom to be, far from a
proper occasion of British self-afflatus, the very
flagship of the modern language.

Yours truly,
Robert L. Moore
New York, N.Y.

November 29, 1985

Memo to our readers:
As we go to press, neither of the two letters below has been published. By
telephone with *Newsweek*, we learn that a "shortened" version of the
letter addressed to it will appear next week (about the same time this

issue reaches our subscribers). *The New York Times* advises that its legal department will need to check the wording of the letter addressed to it. Since all of this takes time, we proceed to scoop *Newsweek* and the *Times*. In due course, our readers will be hearing more from us about the Liberty [sic] Lobby v. National Review case. —WFB

Editor
Newsweek Magazine
444 Madison Avenue
New York, N.Y. 10022

Dear Sirs:

Your item (October 21) entitled "Firing Line in the Courtroom" has got to be a matter of concern for those friends of *Newsweek* who worry about your reputation. You report on a lawsuit between *National Review* (of which I am the editor) and Liberty Lobby (run by Willis Carto) in which you refer to them as "two apostles of conservatism." You conclude by quoting "a Carto ally" as saying, "They [i.e., I and Carto] agree on about 90 per cent of their positions."

That is about as illuminating as if *National Review* were to report that *Newsweek* and the Soviet Union agreed "on about 90 per cent of their positions" (health care, Social Security, educational opportunity for all . . .). What is distinctive about Liberty Lobby isn't its love of the American flag or its belief in the free market. The outstanding contribution of Liberty Lobby to the public discourse is its concern, as its prime mover put it in a letter, for the "niggerfication" of America, and its discovery that the Holocaust is a Jewish hoax. Liberty Lobby was correctly designated in 1982 by the Anti-Defamation League as "the strongest voice of anti-Semitism in America." You also neglected to mention that the District Court dismissed Liberty Lobby's legal complaints against *National Review* as being without merit, and further neglected to note that the same court ruled that two counts of *National Review*'s counterclaim were valid. In short, you did about as much as any journalistic account could possibly do to lose sight entirely of the relevant issues. No doubt your sleepy reporter, if he disdained the breed of combatants, would have reported a lawsuit brought by the Black Panthers against the NAACP as just another nigger-fight.

Yours faithfully,
Wm. F. Buckley Jr.

Editor
The New York Times
229 West 43rd Street
New York, NY 10036

Dear Sirs:

Your story (October 26, page 10) seriously misleads, and that should be a matter of concern for the newspaper of record. Your headline reads, "14-Year Conservative War Ends in Libel Judgment for Magazine." And the lead sentence refers to a quarrel between "two organs of the conservative movement, *National Review* and Liberty Lobby."

I think that on reflection the author of that article would concede that a journal does not qualify as a "conservative organ" merely by pointing out, say, the need for an Army, Navy, Air Force, and national anthem in between references to the Zionist conspiracy and worries by its prime mover over the looming "niggerfication" of America. No more, is my guess, would a journal qualify to be designated merely as a "liberal organ" if it editorialized for free medicine, while defending Stalinism. Liberty Lobby is known to all who have eyes to see as an anti-Semitic tabloid which, at least as far as I am concerned, lies with lascivious regularity. (Did you know that Hitler's Holocaust was a Jewish hoax?) Think what you will of American conservatism, but pray do not confuse it with that pestilential sheet.

Yours faithfully,
Wm. F. Buckley Jr.

February 14, 1986

Dear Bill,

  I can't believe after all I've done for you that you would leave me out of your book, *Right Reason*. I guess when people appear on Johnny Carson's show they forget their roots.

Sincerely,
Art [Buchwald]
Washington, D.C.

Memo to: Bill
From: Priscilla

  I thought you would like to see this tribute to your penmanship from our friend Bob Strother [a veteran journalist living in Mexico].

Dear Priscilla:

  You will be interested to know that when I handed a local handwriting analyst a sample of brother Bill's chirography, she angrily handed it back, declaring that she would not be victimized by a clumsy hoax. It was not the product of a human hand, she said, surmising that it might have been made by a seismograph with the croup. She gave me my dollar back. Of course I defended Bill's penmanship by saying that it was no more difficult than Etruscan, once you decided which side was up.

  My son-in-law's handwriting is a good rival for Bill's. A cryptologist once told him that if François Champollion had decrypted some Helms for practice he

could have saved himself at least six months in
decoding the Rosetta stone.

All best,
Bob
Cuernavaca, Mexico

February 28, 1986

Dear Mr. Buckley:

  Q: How many congressmen does it take to change a
light bulb?
  A: Five hundred thirty-five, but only if the following
conditions are met:
  The light bulb will not be changed in an election
year. A committee will study the light-bulb situation
for at least a year. Taxes will have to be raised. A fair
and proportionate number of the light-bulb changers
will be from minority groups. No Social Security funds
will be used to change the bulb. Each state and
congressional district will share in the benefits of
changing the light bulb. The blame for the failure
of the present bulb will be assigned to the other party.
The new bulb will be twice as bright as the old bulb.
Because the new bulb is twice as bright as the old bulb,
it will cost 130 times as much. A Blue Ribbon Panel will
investigate light-bulb failures and issue a mega-page
report to the Congress. A fact-finding trip to all
countries known to produce light bulbs will be made by
most congressmen and their wives. The CIA will
investigate the Russian light-bulb changing system.
Details of the Russian light-bulb changing system will
be sold to the Chinese by an American naval officer. The
surgeon general will issue a report about the perils of

over-bright light bulbs. A program to supply light
bulbs to those who cannot afford them will be introduced
by Tip O'Neill. President Reagan will give a speech
extolling the virtues of kerosene lanterns. Tip O'Neill
will initiate a program of free kerosene for the needy.

    And finally, each and every congressman will send
every one of his constituents a newsletter describing
how he managed to get the light bulb changed almost
single-handedly.

Darwin R. Crum
Schaumburg, Ill.

*Dear Mr. Crum: Many thanks. I've been worrying about it. I'm glad you've
got it down to the nuts and bolts. You should take on disarmament next.
Cordially, WFB*

March 28, 1986

Dear Mr. Buckley:

    This past week my copy of *NR* and *Sports Illustrated*'s
celebrated "swimsuit issue" arrived simultaneously in
my mail box.

    To my surprise, I found that I read *NR* cover to cover
before examining the *SI*.

    Does this signal that my espousal of conservatism is
now complete?

Sincerely,
Bill Howell
Clarksburg, W.Va.

*Dear Mr. Howell: In part, yes. But it also signals that your espousal of other
things is less than complete. Many thanks. Yours cordially, WFB*

May 9, 1986

```
WFB--
  Quick question. Why is Qaddafi (Quadaffi, Kadafy,
etc.), the megalomaniac Svengali, only a colonel?

Lee Wasserman
Cleveland, Ohio
```

Dear Mr. Wasserman: Maybe because Colonel Qaddafi shot all the generals?
Cordially, WFB

June 20, 1986

```
AND THE PROPHET LOOKED ON THE TEMPTATION OF MALACHEY IN THE
BOOK OF BUCKLEY AND HE SAW THAT IT WAS VERY GOOD.
  STILL, HIS HEART STIRRED WITHIN HIM. HE WAXED WROTH, AND
HE SAID TO THE LORD GOD, "HOW SHALL IT BE, LORD, THAT THIS
SCRIBE SHALL BE SO SMOOTH OF TONGUE THAT HE SHALL HIMSELF
SPEAK TO THE PEOPLE? THAT IS MY TASK, LORD, THAT THOU HAST
LAID UPON ME LONG AGO.
  AND THE LORD SAID UNTO MOSES, "BE THOU FIRM OF SPIRIT. I
AM THE LORD, THY GOD. I KNOW ALL THAT HATH BEEN AND ALL THAT
SHALL COME TO PASS. DO THOU MY BIDDING. WHATSOEVER THY HAND
FINDETH TO DO, THEREFORE DO IT WITH ALL THY MIGHT."
  AND IT WAS SO.

C.
Beverly Hills, Calif.
```

Dear Charlton Heston: If you think you can fool me by trying to play Moses
this side of Hollywood, why you have a surprise coming. By the way, er, what
did . . . He . . . think of my Temptation of Wilfred Malachey *tape? I mean,*
as if you knew. Best, Bill

JOURNALIST-IN-SPACE PROJECT
ASSOCIATION OF SCHOOLS OF
JOURNALISM AND MASS COMMUNICATION

Dear Mr. Buckley,

This is to inform you that your application was not among those selected for further review in the Journalist-in-Space Project.

The one hundred semifinalists, who were selected from more than 1,700 applicants, will be announced on or about April 24. We expect to announce the forty regional nominees from this group in May.

Thank you for your time and your interest. The enclosed certificate recognizes your participation in the Journalist-in-Space Project and is an expression of our sincere appreciation for your support.

Best wishes,
Albert T. Scroggins
Chief Program Officer, College of Journalism
University of South Carolina
Columbia, S.C.

Dear Mr. Scroggins: Okay, okay. So I won't be NR's *first space reporter. Maybe I'll figure out a way to get there first via the private sector, in which case I'll wave. Cordially, WFB*

August 1, 1986

Mr. Michael Kramer
New York Magazine

Dear Mike:

You write (incredibly) in your mag, May 12, "Having neatly rebuked [Charles] Murray, whom he [Daniel Patrick Moynihan, in his book

Disintegration Blues] calls a serious scholar despite Murray's support of William F. Buckley Jr.'s proposal for 'taking away the right to vote from anyone who [has] no source of income except welfare,' Moynihan is less helpful in shaping a future."

I have seen non-sequiturs in my life, baby ones, middle-sized ones, and great big ones, but they all stand aside in awe at yours. A policy recommendation has nothing to do with scholarship, serious or non-serious. And if it did, I take the occasion to remind you that the proposal attributed to me was first made by John Stuart Mill, whose scholarly credentials are generally accepted.

Yours cordially,
Bill

October 24, 1986

Dear Mr. Buckley:

  Horrible day! *NR*, July 4, "The Murder of SALT II," page 15, line 4--"whom" instead of "who." ["SALT II is dead. European governments and popular media throughout the world have convened a kangaroo tribunal to try and pillory the murderer, whom they all agree is the United States (who else?)."] "O passi graviora, dabit deus his quoque finem." Should the cordial editor not?

Nell L. Galloway (Mrs. Ralph)
Cincinnati, Ohio

Dear Mrs. Galloway: You missed the point. We were attempting to use grammatical counterparts for geopolitical solecisms. Everybody else got it! Sadly, WFB

Mr. Buckley:

If the United States Government adopts the policy of comparative worth, will the salaries of congressmen be reduced to those of ribbon clerks, or will the salaries of ribbon clerks be increased to those of congressmen?

Bill Zopf
Jacksonville, Ill.

December 31, 1986

Remarks at a Gala

On November 18, the Ethics and Public Policy Center in Washington, D.C., gave its tenth anniversary dinner, "honoring William F. Buckley Jr., recipient of the Shelby Cullom Davis Award." Testimonials were read from Lech Walesa, Henry Kissinger, Alexander Haig, and Malcolm Muggeridge, who were not present. President Reagan was the first speaker. Excerpts from WFB's remarks follow.

Mr. President, Dr. Lefever,* ladies and gentlemen.

I've never made a screen test, nor been called upon to pass judgment on a screen test, so I think I need to let air out of this wonderful, Montgolfieran balloon by observing that wonderful though you have all been as performers, none of you would meet the requirements of *cinéma vérité* in depicting me as you have. I am greatly blessed in this world, in wonderful ways, notable among them the generosity of my friends. But I think it appropriate privately to confess—the bishops having recently reaffirmed that collective acts of penitence are to be avoided—that in my public life I have in almost every situation pursued my most hedonistic

---

*Ernest Lefever, founder and head of the Ethics and Public Policy Center.

impulses. I suppose it might even be reasoned that I calculated that if he were elected President, then perhaps Ronald Reagan might one day speak at a dinner in which I figured and utter such unforgettable, however unforgivable, compliments as he has uttered here tonight. But the hero, surely, is the man who denies himself. When I argued that Mr. Reagan should be President of the United States, I was much less concerned with the question whether he would enjoy the consummation of his ambition, than with whether I would enjoy the consummation of mine, which was that Mr. Reagan should become President. When over the years I made this point or the other, advocating this policy or the other, I was doing what I wished to do, which is not to be compared with washing the dishes, which I have done, even if memory closes out on when last I did it; or cleaning toilets, which I did from time to time serving in the infantry of the Army of the United States, no doubt leaving my instructors debating the question whether I was better, or worse, at this than at trench warfare.

I guess what I need to say is that however grateful I am for your generosity, I have no illusions of having earned it. I remember as a boy hearing of the young man who applied to the traveling carnival for a job. Asked by the skeptical manager just what he could do, he said that he could dive from a hundred-foot ladder into a barrel of sawdust. The manager was much intrigued by the young supply-side acrobat and ordered the ladder hoisted, from the distant top of which, moments later, the young applicant dived, to the astonishment of wide-eyed attendants, right into the barrel. The excited manager approached him, as the applicant crawled out, dusting himself off, and offered him $100 a week. But catching the expression of a Yankee bargainer, he quickly raised that to $200 and, after much sweat, to the unheard-of sum of $300. He demanded, finally, an explanation of the acrobat's unverbalized shaking of his head. "Well," the young man replied, "you see, before just now, I never did this thing before, and to tell you the truth, I don't like it."

But I do like it. It just happens—I can only think that grace is responsible for this, while also singling me out as a baby who survived my mother's constitutional Freedom to Choose—that I was born inclined toward the service of my own opinions, which, happily, tend to coincide with those of our Founding Fathers and—however inexactly I am guided by them, and deficiently disciplined in exercising them—with those of my Maker. I would deserve a medal if I got up one day and spoke out for progressive taxation, or détente, or protectionism, or socialized medicine for louseworts. But then the medal would come from such people as award them for successful screen tests by those who act out of character.

So I do not exaggerate my gratitude to you all, while quietly reminded of Ambrose Bierce's definition of "admiration" as "Our polite recognition of another's similarity to ourselves." . . .

February 27, 1987

Dear Bill:

   The damnedest thing happened the other day. I received from Hertz a package wrapped in platinum paper. When I opened it, there was the most beautiful leather Cartier wallet. But wait, there's more. In the wallet were ninety one-hundred-dollar bills, plus a Hertz Platinum Service card. I assume you got the same. It's a great club we belong to, particularly since it's so rare that we rent cars.
   See you in the Hertz Club men's bar one of these days.

Cheers,
Art [Buchwald]
Washington, D.C.

Dear Art: I wouldn't be proud of those ninety one-hundred-dollar bills. That means Hertz thinks you're for sale. I got the wallet and the Platinum card, but no bills. They know I'm not for sale. They know I'm a conservative, and you're— Let's go somewhere one of these days in a Hertz. Shall we use your card or your cash? Cordially, Bill

June 5, 1987

Dear Mr. Buckley:

Re your *Firing Line* interview with Henry Kissinger, from a qualified TV professional objective concerned American: The manner in which you sit is rude. Can't you sit upright in an adult fashion? In single shots you appear tilted. In two shots you sit as if your guest has BO.

1. Even in questioning you appear rude. You don't ask questions of a guest (even one whose opinion you favor) but your questions come in a long form of interrogation.

2. You always come up with the personal insecurity of a long preface attempting to show what you know.

3. Finally, we have tried the Liberal Way and it has not worked. We have tried the Conservative Road, and neither has that worked, although Conservatives are still attempting to force a square peg into a round hole.

Sincerely,
Hamilton Morgen
Harrison, N.Y.

P.S.: In my book, the professed Liberals and Conservatives have been the most anti-American.

Dear Mr. Morgen: 1) No, I can't sit upright. Congenital. Most people don't talk about it out loud! 2) If you think my questions are long, try Socrates. 3) Of course I want to share what I know about the subject: after all, I spent three hours reading up on it the night before. Have you ever jumped out of an airplane at midnight with a parachute? With the mission of eliminating the guard at the end of a bridge? Well, I haven't either, but if I did, I would certainly want detailed up-front instructions. 4) The trick, Morgen, when you run into that problem, is to make the hole a little larger in diameter—and plop!, in goes the square peg. Cordially, WFB

P.S.: In which of your books?

July 3, 1987

Dear Mr. Buckley:

Perhaps this letter should more appropriately have been sent to "Dear Abby." In any event, I am having domestic problems with my wife and desperately need your advice.

It all started when she neglected to pay my *National Review* subscription for several months because she thought she had already paid it. In reality, she had paid the bill for my *New Republic* subscription, and did not realize that there was any difference between the two magazines.

I am a compassionate man and as a Christian was capable of forgiving her for this error. Last week, however, she committed a heinous act. She videotaped something called *Pee Wee Herman's Playhouse* over a portion of my *Firing Line* collection. Do I have any recourse besides divorce?

I anxiously await your reply.

Very truly yours,
Patrick J. Courtney
Somers, Conn.

Dear Mr. Courtney: On the general point, your wife has used up only two of her seventy × seven ration and therefore has a long way to go. On the particular point, which episode of Pee Wee Herman *replaced which episode of* Firing Line? *I can think of a dozen episodes of* Firing Line *I'd welcome replacing with an hour of Bela Lugosi, let alone Pee Wee (whoever he is). Cordially, WFB*

July 17, 1987

Dear Bill:

   Thank you so much for the ride to the airport. When I got back to my office this questionnaire from Hertz was waiting for me. I was wondering if you could fill it out for me and send it in, as you have much more feel for what the Platinum Service people want when they question you.

Cheers,
Art [Buchwald]
Washington, D.C.

Dear Art: Done. You certainly travel well. Let me know when next you need a ride from the airport. Cordially, Bill

January 22, 1988

Dear Mr. Buckley:

   One who prefers lexipenia is called lexipeniac. Could you please tell me what you call one who uses logorrhea?

Sincerely,
Andrew A. Ponaras
Lake Worth, Fla.

Dear Mr. Ponaras: The word you are searching for is "wordy." Cordially, WFB

February 19, 1988

Editor
The Spectator
56 Doughty Street
London WC1N 2LL
England

Sirs:

Your issue of 2 January has just reached these shores. I read in it Mr. Peregrine Worsthorne's diary, as charming as it was apocryphal, composed as though he had spent a long night out with Taki. He writes that it is not "immediately obvious" to him why Mr. John O'Sullivan is leaving Downing Street "to edit a fairly obscure, right-wing American magazine." The obvious reason is captured in the adage, "Tous les beaux esprits se rencontrent"—in the spirit of Anglo-American comity, it is only fair that Mrs. Thatcher should share the hugely talented Mr. O'Sullivan with us, and only natural that he should move from the eudaemonistic center of Great Britain to its counterpart in the United States. On the other matter, I don't quite know how Mr. O'Sullivan, as my deputy, can make *National Review* less obscure. Ours is the leading journal of opinion in the United States (circulation 122,000). At our Thirtieth Anniversary celebration a couple of years ago, the guests included the President of the United States and four members of his Cabinet. At our Twentieth Anniversary celebration, the principal speaker was Professor Michael Oakeshott, who, at Cambridge, once taught Mr. Worsthorne, though not quite enough.

Yours truly,
Wm. F. Buckley Jr.

May 13, 1988

Frank A. Olson
Chairman
The Hertz Corporation

Dear Frank,

Thank you so much for sending me the Christmas card
wishing me and my Hertz Platinum Card a Merry Christmas
and a prosperous New Year.

I heard through the grapevine that you gave Bill
Buckley a seat on the New York Stock Exchange for
having driven ten thousand miles in one of your cars.
I was curious whether you are handing these out to all
Platinum Service clients, or just to Buckley because
of his television show. Buckley is always one-upping
me and I was wondering if he invented the tale of the
Stock Exchange seat to get me mad.

Sincerely,
Art [Buchwald]
Washington, D.C.

DEAR MR. OLSON: GOT YOUR SELL ORDER. HERTZCO, 1,000,000 SHARES.
FLOOR GOING CRAZY, HAVING A WONDERFUL TIME, LET'S DO SOME-
THING ONE OF THESE DAYS FOR ART, WHAT DO YOU SAY? BUCKLEY

Dear Mr. Buckley:

The declining value of the dollar has created a once-
in-a-lifetime opportunity to build your export business
at *National Review*. Specifically, Mr. Buckley, in reviewing
your computer database analysis of the major exporters in
the New York area, I did not find an extensive amount of
activity in the area of export at *National Review*.

I have some specific ideas on how you can enhance the export of your products. We are one of America's leading export consultant companies, serving small businesses and Fortune 500 companies alike. Please call me and I will arrange to meet with you and one of your senior executives.

Very truly yours,
Harold X. Saunders
Great Neck, N.Y.

Dear Mr. Saunders: Thanks. We would like to increase our exports to the Soviet Union and await your advice on how to proceed. Cordially, WFB

May 27, 1988

Dear Mr. Buckley:

In Robert Dornan's wonderful article, "Stop Beating around the Bush" [Nov. 6], he made a slight error when he said that whereas Bush has been referred to as a preppy, you--a fellow Yalie--have not.

On the contrary, *The Official Preppy Handbook* (Lisa Birnbach, Workman Publishing, 1980) lists you under the Prep Pantheon.

"William F. Buckley Jr.--St. Thomas More and St. John's, Beaumont (England), and Millbrook, Yale '50. Author, critic, publisher, television personality. Earned an immediate place in Prep Pantheon for his first book, *God and Man at Yale*. Would have made it anyway for his patrician demeanor, number 2 pencil, and amazing curling tongue."

You are listed along with John Adams, George Bush, F. Scott Fitzgerald, Katharine Hepburn, George Plimpton, Elliot Richardson, Clare Boothe Luce, Cole

Porter, Grace Kelly, and the members of the
architectural firm of McKim, Mead, and White. Wow!
(There are others too numerous to mention here.)
    You are also cited as a reference on how to speak
like a preppy. Your accent is referred to as New
England Nasal Nip.

Sincerely,
Kimberly J. Gustin
Indianapolis, Ind.

*Dear Miss Gustin: Don't use a pencil, haven't for fifty years. Nasal Nip
accent result of chronic sinus. When you fly, one Seldane morning and night,
day before flight, day of flight, day after flight; one Sudafed two hours before
flight; Afrin nose drops just before and just after take-off; Ayr during flights;
one Actifed one hour before landing; try that to avoid sounding like
Your servant, WFB*

October 14, 1988

Dear Mr. Buckley:

    I was reading in *U.S. News* the other day and it said
that Michael Dukakis is a "post-liberal Democrat."
I'm somewhat confused by this nomenclature, because
he still seems like a liberal to me. What does
"post-liberal" mean when applied to a liberal?
    Is he a "post-liberal liberal"? No, that sounds
stupid. How about "pragmatic liberal"? No, that's an
oxymoron. I'm confused. Help me out.

Earnestly,
E. Dale Franks Jr.
APO N.Y.

Dear Mr. Franks: A "post-liberal" Democrat adopts present liberal programs festooned with non-liberal rhetoric. Thus, Mr. Dukakis will a) hugely increase state benefits, while b) hugely diminishing state expenditures. Cordially, WFB

November 7, 1988

Dear Mr. Buckley:

I have always thought that a picture of you, placed next to my picture of the President and Jack Kemp, would perfect my bedroom. I never knew how I could get one until recently, while watching coverage of the New York gay-rights march, I saw one of the lesbian liberators carrying your image. This struck me as being a bit (pardon the pun) queer. Upon further inspection, however, I observed a caption that read "William F. Buckley Jr., Public Enemy." If one of these Looney Leftists could obtain a poster of you, then why couldn't I? So, I am hereby beseeching you to aid me in my quest for your picture. The one on the cover of *Right Reason* is my favorite.

Cordially,
David Abrami
Orlando, Fla.

Dear Mr. Abrami: One of the ways to get my picture as on Right Reason *is to buy a copy of* Right Reason. *Or, you could join the lesbians. But, to spare you either indignity, I will send along a copy. Cordially, WFB*

February 24, 1989

Dear Bill:

I think we have been ignoring what is truly a serious ethical problem. Are we, as holders of the Hertz

Platinum Service card, part of the conspiracy to cheat Hertz clients through insurance and damage-claim fraud?

These costs have affected every man, woman, and child in the United States, and driven many into poverty and ruin. I frankly don't give a damn. If you feel the same way, let's just continue being members and refuse to be interviewed on *60 Minutes,* if they ask us.

If Hertz customers are so stupid and don't check their bills, I do not see why we should go to bat for them. I am sick and tired of so many consumers who have turned into chronic complainers.

Cheers,
Art [Buchwald]
Washington, D.C.

Dear Art: You are right, as usual. The idea of turning complaints against Hertz into an excuse for voting for Dukakis makes me sick and tired, and when that happens, I get so angry I eat my latest Hertz card. Yours, Bill

March 1, 1989

Memo to: WFB
From: McF*

Bill, hanc scriptum vidisti?

From *Fort Pierce* (Fla.) *Tribune,* Q&A column by editor Lee Barnes. "Why don't you print William F. Buckley's political columns?" "We have a policy here that we will only use columnists who write in English."

McF: Qualis anus equi! —Bill

---

*Jim McFadden, *NR*'s associate publisher.

July 14, 1989

Dear Mr. Buckley:

I'm worried about my mother.

Three years ago, I gave her a gift subscription to *National Review*. Now, she's speaking in tongues. Specifically, Latin tongues. I'm afraid *NR*'s Latinists are getting to her.

For example, she recently spoke these words of wisdom to me: "Populus iamdudum defutatus est." She said this means: "The people have been getting screwed long enough." Assuming the political (rather than the biological) connotations of this, I couldn't agree more. But is it proper for such a dignified lady, the former Pickle Queen of Wiggins, Mississippi, to be speaking like a commoner?

I feel honored to have inhabited the same century as two of history's grandest ladies: Clare Boothe Luce and Alice Roosevelt Longworth. One of them (I can't remember which) once proclaimed: "I'm in the springtime of my senility." Could this be happening to my mother?

Don C. Lynch
Baton Rouge, La.

Dear Mr. Lynch: We hope not. She sounds bright and full of verve at this end. Cordially, WFB

Dear Mr. Buckley:

Nietzsche said: "What does not kill me makes me stronger." Was he right? Had he ever seen a pickup truck?

Sincerely,
Robert Faltin
Edmonton, Alberta

Dear Mr. Faltin: a) No, Nietzsche (1844–1900) hadn't ever seen a pickup truck; and b) No, he wasn't right (TB doesn't always kill, but it leaves you weaker); and c) Try your questions next door. What do you think we poor people at NR are, Information Please? Cordially, WFB

August 18, 1989

Memo to: Bill
From: Frances [Bronson]

Here's a letter from the Letterman people. It speaks for itself. Let me know your decision.

NBC ENTERTAINMENT
LATE NIGHT WITH DAVID LETTERMAN

Dear Miss Bronson:

Here is a script for a possible William Buckley cameo on *Late Night with David Letterman*. The script should be more or less self-explanatory but if you have any questions, don't hesitate to ask.

If he's willing to do it, we would like to schedule it at his earliest convenience. This segment would be at the very first part of the show, which we tape from 5:30 to 6:30, so it wouldn't require too much of his time.

I'll give you a call to see what you all think. I hope we can work something out.

Best regards,
Maria Pope
Writers' Segment Coordinator

Script for possible WILLIAM BUCKLEY cameo
LATE NIGHT WITH DAVID LETTERMAN
PAUL GETS HELP WITH CHAT WITH DAVE

After Dave does his opening remarks and crosses back to homebase, he sits at the desk and begins his usual chat with Paul. Paul interrupts.

PAUL: Dave, I know this is the part of the show where we ad lib a fascinating repartee . . .

DAVE: I suppose you could call it that . . . Or, you could call it "dead air."

PAUL: I was feeling a little tired tonight so I thought instead I'd get someone to fill in for me just this once. OK?

DAVE: Sure, I guess so, if you're really bushed.

PAUL: Let me bring him out here . . . a brilliant conversationalist--William Buckley! *(William Buckley comes out and stands at Paul's mike.)*

WILLIAM BUCKLEY: Hello, Dave. Tell me, how was your weekend?

DAVE: Very good. How was your weekend, William?

WILLIAM BUCKLEY: Fantastic.

PAUL: Ladies and gentlemen . . . William Buckley!

Buckley exits to thunderous applause, and Dave, having satisfied a talk show's need for a little inane chatter at the start, proceeds as usual . . .

Frances: Okay. —B.

September 15, 1989

Mr. James Fallows
Boston, Mass.

Dear Mr. Fallows:

The Best of Business Quarterly for Summer 1989 quotes you as follows:

"Americans acquire the patina of old money by pretending that they are Englishmen. William F. Buckley Jr. has basically the same lineage as, say, Lyndon Johnson. Johnson was descended from rural Texas politicians, and so is Buckley, whose grandfather was a sheriff in south Texas. But instead of wearing a cowboy hat and leisure suit, like Johnson, Buckley made himself sound as if he were a tenth-generation Old Etonian. In a sense, he is the classic American, since he has completely invented a new identity for himself."

You should know that the invention of myself as a tenth-generation Old Etonian required a great deal of planning. I (and my four younger siblings) spoke only Spanish at home (my parents had lived in Mexico after they were married). At age three, I went to my first school—in Paris, where the language is French, even among the nouveaux. I was exposed to English for the first time in London at age five, when I was enrolled in the Blessed Sir Thomas More School. From there I went to New England and, at age 12, back to England to a boarding school (St. John's, Beaumont, six miles from Eton) (by the way, if you think I speak with an Eton accent, you don't know an Eton accent); then to boarding school in the Hudson Valley. During this period I visited Texas twice, once for three days, once for two days. But then the affinity between Lyndon Johnson and my grandfather was certainly strong: although my grandfather died in 1904, he voted for Johnson in 1948.

Having quoted you on the subject, I do hope you know more about the production of F-16s than you do about the production of Buckleys. If not, you should write about other things.

Yours truly,
Wm. F. Buckley Jr.

September 29, 1989

Dear Mr. Buckley:

Just a note in passing on flag burning. If it ever again becomes a crime, I propose the following. Since most of the brain-damaged charmers who torch Old Glory are lovers of Communism, I submit that they be sentenced to six months' use of Russian toilet paper. I guarantee that at the end of that time something will be on fire, but it will not be the American flag.

Cordially yours,
Fred Fierthaler
Nineveh, N.Y.

Dear Mr. Fierthaler: Interesting point. That would certainly take care of the relevant end of the flag burners. Cordially, WFB

February 5, 1990

Memo to: WFB
From: Rick [Brookhiser]*

When we [the *NR* staff] went to Beaverkill for our management retreat, I left some clothes in a drawer. They got sent to the wrong address. The attached correspondence shows what ensued.

THOMAS B. COCHRAN, PHD
SENIOR SCIENTIST
NATURAL RESOURCES DEFENSE COUNCIL
WASHINGTON, D.C.

Dear Mr. Brookhiser:

Your dirty drawers are being sent to you by the staff of the NRDC, where they were sent by mistake by the

---

*A senior editor of *National Review*.

Beaverkill Inn. If you would like to protect your shorts and the environment, make a small contribution to our organization--application enclosed.

T. B. Cochran

Dear Mr. Cochran:

And in return, why not subscribe to *National Review*, where I work? Other magazines only hang out the nation's dirty linen. We send it to you.

Sincerely,
Richard Brookhiser

Dear Rick: Fun. Cochran sounds like a grump. If he is one of our natural resources, he too needs laundering. —Bill

March 5, 1990

Dear Bill:

I guess that Hertz had a bad year--all I got was the jet plane. I am enclosing a picture of it. You would think that when you are a Platinum Card member they'd come up with something with more engines. I guess the thing to do is just accept it and not make a big fuss.

If you need a ride, let me know.

Cheers,
Art [Buchwald]
Washington, D.C.

Dear Art: I got an airplane too, but thanks anyway for the offer of a ride on yours. Now that you own Hollywood, maybe you should think of sending Mr. Hertz a present at Christmastime? Warmest, Bill

April 16, 1990

WNET, Channel 13
356 West 58th Street
New York, N.Y. 10019

Re: Program *Firing Line*, Saturday, 10 A.M.,
Wm. F. Buckley Jr.

   I happen to have always liked, enjoyed, and
respected William Buckley till I started watching
him on TV. I think he would be better on radio--his
knowledge would come through but one would not
have to look at:
   1) an ill-fitting shirt,
   2) crooked tie,
   3) slouching sitting/lying position (as if he were
suffering from hemorrhoids).
   Also, he is constantly scratching his head with his
pen/pencil and then he puts it in his mouth.
   Does he not have a wife, mother, or sweetheart who
could straighten him out???
   For a millionaire, he is a mess!!! The program and
guests are *great*, but I cannot look.

Sincerely,
Antonette Benson
Syosset, N.Y.

*Dear Miss Benson: Don't you understand? I do all that in order to distract
from the hypnotic quality of my reasoning. Otherwise my points of view
would overwhelm the public, and that would be the end of* Firing Line.
Cordially, WFB

June 11, 1990

Dear Mr. Buckley:

The moment I saw that *Time* magazine selected Mikhail Gorbachev as "Man of the Decade" (for doing what Ronald Reagan's policies forced him to do), the perfect analogy came to mind.

If a miracle drug is ever discovered that cures all disease, *Time* magazine will honor disease.

Cordially,
Andrew Turnbull
Epsom, N.H.

Right on, Turnbull! Disease of the Century! Cordially, WFB

July 23, 1990

To the Editor
The Spectator
London

Dear Sirs:

Mr. Simon Sebag-Montefiore was obviously sustained by mountainous predilections when he interviewed me (*Spectator*, May 19, 1990), and I haven't the time or the inclination to reorient him. Three things caught my eye, however, that merit attention. 1) He quotes me, by which I mean he puts inside quotation marks the sentence: "I know [Mrs. Thatcher] well. She has been on my show many times." a) I don't know Mrs. Thatcher well; b) she hasn't been on my show "many times" (she has been on twice); and, while I am at it, c) if I did know her well and if she had been on my show "many times" I wouldn't have said so in those words. Such formulations don't generate in me.

2) Mr. S-M writes, "He is as famous for his sailing books, detective novels, and tales of his own socialite life as he is for his politics. In 1983's Overdrive, for example, he describes his Jacuzzi as the 'most beautiful indoor pool since Pompeii.'" Sorry, but how did that "for example" get in there? For example of what? In fact, my pool (not my Jacuzzi) is probably the most beautiful indoor pool since Pompeii.

And finally, 3) your correspondent writes that "the name of the novel that made him famous when he was only 24 [was] God and Man at Yale." To write that God and Man at Yale was a novel is on the order of writing that *Lucky Jim* is an account of the life of James II. But the young man was in an awful hurry, and clearly doesn't have the advantage of restoring himself at night in the most beautiful indoor pool since Pompeii.

Yours faithfully,
Wm. F. Buckley Jr.

Dear Mr. Buckley:

 Can you riddle me this? Several days ago I received unexpectedly a check from the U.S. Treasury for $1,000 marked "Tax Ref." They said they will soon (!) send me a complete explanation. However, if I "cash the check and it is later determined that I was not entitled to it I may be charged interest from the date of the refund to the date of repayment."

 Needless to say I won't touch the check and be in a position of paying for the Treasury's mistake. What a way to run etc.

Sincerely,
Howard Benoist Jr.
St. Louis, Mo.

Dear Mr. Benoist: Why don't you turn the check over to *National Review*? We'll send three subscriptions to the Kennedy, Johnson, and Carter Libraries, which are tax deductible; and then let them figure it out. Meanwhile, we'll indemnify you. Cordially, WFB

December 17, 1990

Dear Mr. Buckley:

  You put the news media on a pedestal when you continually refer to them as "the media." Remember, there are other media: transportation, advertising, and even communications. At least conservative *National Review* should not revere the liberals--their doing it themselves is already too much.

Cordially,
Mickey McArthur
Sonoita, Ariz.

Dear Mr. McArthur: Don't follow you, sorry. We review the media the way pigeons review statues. (Original: W. Sheed.) Cordially, WFB

January 28, 1991

To the Editor
The New Republic

Dear Sir:

  One or two points, if I may, to clarify misunderstandings that might have been generated by Mr. Kaus's review (Dec. 31) of my book *Gratitude*.
  He notes that I am hospitable to the use of government sanctions to induce enrollment in national service and wonders how such sanctions could corral the affluent young. "For them Buckley holds out the cute

coercion of the loss of a driver's license (why not deny them electricity, while we're at it?) and the prospect of unspecified 'auxiliary sanctions' to be applied by individual states. Buckley says he's not statist; he's just a stateist."

I wrote (p. 138), "In order to achieve such a goal [voluntary national service] it is important to lean on the moral sanctions. What is needed is a conscious mobilization of social, philanthropic, and civic enthusiasm for the idea of national service." On the business of why not deny them electricity one has to ask just who, really, is being cute. In Arkansas, the denial of a driver's license has the endorsement of the Democratic governor and of the relevant committee heads of the legislature, a sanction designed for those who drop out of high school. If society should come to deem exposure to civic enterprise as being as critical a waystation to responsible citizenship as one more year of secondary school and votes an equivalent sanction against that dropout, Mr. Kaus will then worry whether cutting off the electricity is the next draconian step.

On Mr. Kaus's point that if there is work that needs doing, taxes should be levied to do it, my book seeks to make plain that the very idea of civic-mindedness and philanthropy is to get done things that aren't properly the business of the state to subsidize by redistribution. To be sure, a focus on the whole question of what is properly the business of the state illuminates the frontier, even if it is wobbly, that separates the liberal from the conservative, Mr. Kaus from me. Those who have difficulty with the presumption against the nationalization of concern will have difficulty in understanding the concept of voluntary national service.

And finally, a stylistic point. "Within pages . . . he's back to speechwriting. When he says he wants 'a national morale at home reaching as high as the Alps,' you sense that he's given up." If I had written that sentence to describe what I wished for the United States, Mr. Kaus would have been entitled to his wisecrack. But I was talking about Switzerland and its compulsory draft: "It gives that republic relative military invincibility. But something quite other, it can be plausibly argued, developed: a national cohesion. A sense of civic responsibility. A constant reminder of the need to make sacrifices.

A national morale at home reaching as high as the Alps." When you adduce the Alps in the context of Switzerland you are not injecting the speechmaker's steroids into a metaphor. "As American as apple pie" is okay, "as French as apple pie" is not okay, and one hopes that those who graduate from national service will grow ears that remark the difference; which reminds me to say in conclusion that I truly don't understand Mr. Kaus's suggestion that to preserve books that will otherwise rot in the Library of Congress is the equivalent of pyramid-building. I never suggested that no one would ever consult such books in years to come, and my concern for them is not self-serving, given my conviction that my own books will reside in the Smithsonian.

Yours faithfully,
Wm. F. Buckley Jr.

April 1, 1991

Dear Bill:

  Thank you so much for the book, which just arrived. I intend to read it in my Hertz limousine on the way to Palm Beach. You certainly amaze me with your production. I cannot believe that you manage to do all these things and still keep up with the Valet Parking at LaGuardia.

Cheers,
Art [Buchwald]
Washington, D.C.

Dear Art: Thanks for your concern for the Valet Parking, but not to worry. Supply-side is looking after it. Did you know that Hertz cars are automatically insured if you pay with an American Express card? Try it. I'll hold one for you at Valet Parking, LaGuardia. Warmest, Bill

Dear Mr. Buckley:

   When Saddam Hussein, the Sword of Islam, suddenly withdrew, did we then have Kuwaitus interruptus?

Best regards,
Chris Moran
Chicago, Ill.

Dear Mr. Moran: Ho ho ho. Very nice. Wish I had your Rorschach! Cordially, WFB

April 15, 1991

Dear Mr. Buckley,

   Mr. Gorbachev has put me at a loss for words. He has let Europe go, but he continues with the repression of the Soviet peoples. The linguistic temptation is to say, "The cold war continues, but it is less cold." Yet that leaves us closer to a "hot" conflict in contradistinction to which is the notion of a "cold war." So perhaps we should say, "The cold war has grown colder," but I think that misleading as well. I am at a loss.

Cordially,
Joseph S. Fulda
New York, N.Y.

Dear Mr. Fulda: Not an easy one, no sir. How about: The cold war has, here and there, frozen? Cordially, WFB

June 10, 1991

Dear Mr. Buckley:

  Don't start a sentence with "and." In the last
paragraph of your column I see this, and apparently
the *Star-Ledger* proofreader did not. (She sleeps
a lot.)

  I am beginning to wonder just how good (or bad)
your high school was, and how good (or bad) a student
you were.

Very truly yours,
David Dearborn Jr.
Elizabeth, N.J.

*Dear Mr. Dearborn: Verses 2–26 and 28–31, Chapter I, Genesis, all begin
with "And." The King James scholars went to pretty good high schools.
Cordially, WFB*

July 29, 1991

Dear Mr. Buckley:

  A relevant point is that the King James scholars were
translating the Hebrew vowel *vav*, with which these
verses begin. That vowel is often used as a conjunction,
in which cases it should be translated as "and." In
these verses, however, and characteristically in many
passages in the Bible, *vav* has a different grammatical
function: that of indicating a change in the tense of
the verb. Thus, the phrase that could be literally
translated as "And God will say: Let there be light,"
should be rendered "God said: Let there be light."

  Since the King James translators chose instead to
translate the *vav* that signifies tense change literally

as the conjunction "and," their authority for your use of "and" at the opening of sentences is debatable.

This does not impugn the quality of the high schools they attended. Martin Buber, in the translation of the Bible he carried out with the collaboration of Franz Rosenzweig and Nahum Glatzer, began these sentences with the German *und*. Then, in the final year of his life, Buber decided to rectify this. He eliminated each and every *und* at the beginning of sentences that had translated a *vav* marking a tense change.

Are there not other well educated persons you can claim as the source for the high scholarly right to begin a sentence with an "and," without invoking the ambiguities of deciphering divine language?

Yours sincerely,
David Sidorsky
New York, N.Y.

Dear Mr. Sidorsky: Thank you for your erudite note. But my point wasn't that the King James scholars correctly translated from the original, rather that they were the most influential writers in English history. The general rule is not to begin a sentence with "and"; the particular rule is that writers with a good ear know when to break the general rule. Cordially, WFB

Dear Bill:

The expression "hoist with his own petard" is used by *NR* with sufficient frequency as to approach triteness. Why the hell "hoist," a perfectly useful verb never meant to connote injury?

Sincerely,
Victor R. Matous
Seattle, Wash.

Dear Vic: Aren't you confusing this with heist? And there is certainly an injury to the victim there, unless he was heisted by his own petard. Cordially, WFB

August 12, 1991

Wm--

In "Notes & Asides" [July 29] I see that "hoist with his own petard" causes Mr. Matous some difficulty, as "heist" does you. The two words are etymologically identical, being the past participle of *hoise*, to lift (O.D. hyssen, Fr. hausser, L.L. altiare, L. altus). Heise and heist were dialectic and Scots variants, and the pronunciation heist is identified as archaic although Mencken reports it in standard use in the coal mines of southern Illinois and in "common speech" along with such birds of paradise as clumb, flang, and attackted. Grose (1823) explains how hoist/heist became involved in thievery: "to go upon the hoist; to get into windows accidentally left open: this is done by the assistance of a confederate, called the hoist, who leans his head against the wall, making his back a kind of step or ascent." The metaphor of lifting as stealing is very ancient, by the way: shoplifter makes use of Gothic hlifan to steal (cf. hlifus thief), and I agree with Partridge that the ancestry of lift/hlifan goes back through L. clepo/cleptum, to steal, Gk. klepto as in maniac. The petard (or petar, as it often occurs in an archaic form in the quote from *Hamlet*) was a large can of explosives touched off against a wall to make a breach. The smoke of the sulphurous mixture must have been more than half asphyxiating, to judge from petard's ancestry: peter, to break wind, L. pedo pedere pepidi. Concerning this

derivation I recall that a partner in the brokerage
house where I worked in the late 1950s once used the
"hoist with his own petar" phrase and, when I quizzed
him about it, blushed a deep and desperate red. He
must have gone so far as peter on looking the word up
in his dictionary and not understood that it was
French. He said, with many a hum and haw: "Well,
strung up by his own peter, you see? And it must have
been awfully painful!" So much for Wall Street. As a
sailor you surely know that hawser like hoise comes
from Fr. hausser and so on, and not from any rope
factory. A kissin' cousin is the lovely enhance
(L.L. inaltiare), about which . . . but I have to go
weed the corn patch.

Pretty much yrs. as ever,
Wm [F. Rickenbacker]
[Francestown, N.H.]

August 26, 1991

Dear Bill:

   I would just like you to see the warm letters that
Hertz is now sending out to its Platinum Card members
[letter from the president of Hertz enclosed]. I know
that it will choke you up, but I thought there might be
a book in it. If it could be a movie I, of course, would
write it.
   They don't make people like Frank Olson any more.

Cheers,
Art [Buchwald]
Washington, D.C.

Dear Art: I will write the introduction to your book, and Mr. Olson will put one in each Hertz, and we'll be rich, and won't need to write any more. On the other hand, I don't want to go without reading you, so cancel all the above. Cordially, Bill

Dear Mr. Buckley:

  Please be assured that there is not now, nor has there ever been, a rule against beginning a sentence with *and*, although there have been a good many admonitions to that effect by soi-disant arbiters of usage. Most of this nonsense originated among the late Victorians and their turn-of-the-century successors (but not including the brothers Fowler).
  This silliness survives in some high schools, apparently, but not, I should think, in the better ones. Surely, one of the characteristics of a good high school is that it teaches its students to pay attention to what they read. Anyone who believes that there is a "rule" against beginning a sentence with *and*, or with any other coordinating conjunction, simply isn't paying attention.
  To convince yourself that I'm telling the truth, all you need do is grab the first half-dozen books at hand and begin turning pages at random. You'll quickly find examples in good plenty of sentences beginning with *and*.

Sincerely yours,
Douglas Crenshaw
Antioch, Tenn.

P.S. To save you some trouble, I herewith append some examples culled from the books nearest my own hand. In the event that these fellows aren't sufficiently authoritative for Mr. Sidorsky to acknowledge your "high scholarly right to begin a sentence with an 'and,'" I also append examples from a longer list I keep for another purpose (including sentences from the prose of Wordsworth, Coleridge, Shelley, Lamb, Hazlitt, De Quincey, Carlyle, Mill, Dickens, George Eliot, Arnold, Newman, Ruskin, T. H. Huxley, Pater, Wilde, Shaw, Conrad, Yeats, Joyce, Lawrence, T. S. Eliot, Beckett, Forster, Woolf, Lessing, Hulme, Richards, and Empson). After all, high scholars shouldn't be denied rights everybody else has.

1. And then the fog rose from the ground and from the very leaves, and through the fog I saw the body. --William Goyen, "In the Icebound Hothouse"

2. And the strategy worked. --Paul Johnson, *Intellectuals*

3. And would you write "The worst tennis player around here is I" or "The worst tennis player around here is me"? The first is good grammar, the second is good judgment, although the me might not do in all contexts. --Strunk & White, *Elements of Style*

4. And, for a good fisherman, the object was not to bring home a mess of fish. --Franklin Burroughs, *Billy Watson's Croker Sack*

5. And although it is arguable that a faction might insinuate itself into the control of a legislature, this will be the less likely in proportion to the greater size of the area represented. --Max Beloff, introduction, *The Federalist*

6. And a further reason for caution, in this respect, might be drawn from the reflection, that we are not always sure that those who advocate the truth

```
are actuated by purer principles than their
antagonists. --The Federalist (#1, Hamilton)
   7. And what inspired guesses there have been!--Malcolm
Muggeridge, Confessions of a Twentieth-Century Pilgrim
   8. And wearily, but not simply wearily, he returned
that look.--John Barth, The Last Voyage of Somebody
the Sailor
```

Crenshaw! Stop! I can't stand any more, and you have sent along 62! Massive retaliation was repealed at the Summit last week. Cordially, WFB

September 9, 1991

We Won

In the first issue of *National Review*, published on November 19, 1955, we announced that we were "irrevocably" at war against Communism, and that we would oppose any substitute for victory. Thirty-six years later, Communism was banned within the Soviet Union.

It was a very long haul, and although Richard Nixon, writing a year ago and perhaps anticipating the delirious events of the last ten days in August 1991, was substantially correct when he said that the West didn't win the war, the Communists lost it, that verdict has to be qualified to make room for major and minor players. Where, to drop perhaps the biggest single name of them all, would we have been without Aleksandr Solzhenitsyn? He and a dozen other major figures from the Soviet Union earned their places in Freedom's House of Lords. The crowds in Russia, descendants of the men and women who stormed the Winter Palace, placed themselves between the Soviet tanks and the White House that sheltered Boris Yeltsin, and pledged their lives and their sacred honor to preserving the fetus of Russian constitutionalism. And they prevailed.

In the West there were, everywhere, steadfast friends of liberty, but by no means can it be said that they dominated the public policy of the West.

That can be said of only one figure. It was Ronald Reagan, history is sure to confirm, who suddenly forced the leaders of Soviet Communism to look in the mirror, and what they beheld was their advanced emaciation. The other superpower, thought to have been castrated by the defeat in Vietnam, was deploying theater nuclear weapons in Europe, shattering any prospect of Soviet political ultimatums directed at Bonn, Paris, and London. Moreover, the leader of the bourgeois world was determined to launch a program which the technological genius of America would almost certainly permit absolutely to frustrate a Soviet first strike, and therefore any political advantage that might accrue from threatening such a strike. It was, moreover, the same leader who had resurrected the moral argument, so successfully etiolated by a generation of ambiguists. He spoke of the Soviet Union as an *evil empire*! He said that history would consign Communism to the ash heap of history: transforming Lenin's own words as an ode to historical determinism!

And then, quickly, it began to take over. The war in Afghanistan, never mind that 1.4 million resisters had been killed, was not ending, and the same American President had authorized the use of a weapon that vitiated the usefulness of the Soviet air force. The economy was ceasing to move. A new Soviet leader, having recognized that Afghanistan would not be conquered, attempted to revive the morale of a deadened culture with injections of freedom, and its results were magical, the whole Soviet thinking world suddenly heard from, intoxicated by the glasnost license. Structural reforms were, if not permitted, at least debated. The final failure of the long design to overcome Western Europe, frustrated now by American nuclear missiles, vitiated the importance of continuing military colonization of Eastern Europe; and one after another these nations peeled off. The debated reforms brought a crisis, the sentiment hardening all over the land that there had to be not talk about reforms, but reforms; and on the eve of the first important one of these, a reconstitution of the Union of Soviet Socialist Republics, the dissenters raised their mailed fist in a final show of defiance. Within 48 hours, the mandarinate that controlled the principal instruments of force, the KGB and the military, fell.

We would learn that the eight leaders who sought to stem the tide were, during most of these critical hours, drunk on vodka. They had for most of their lives been intoxicated by more noxious drugs. Before the end of the week, the Communist Party was legally suspended.

We won.

I am uniquely situated to summon the memory of men and women associated with this journal, whose birth was substantially motivated by the historical calling for a moral-analytical journalistic distillery to animate the resistance to Communism. Mr. Nixon was right. We should have won the war against Communism before Yalta's first anniversary, and he was right in suggesting the many lost opportunities which, had we moved otherwise, might have spared millions their lives, and tens of millions those years of the terrible, empty grief that oppression brings. But this was the journal that James Burnham spent 25 years with. It was here that Whittaker Chambers came, however briefly, back to life, after pronouncing that in leaving Communism he had probably left the winning side. It was here that John Dos Passos, and Max Eastman, and Frank Meyer—I restrict myself to those men and women who are dead—labored, in this heady vineyard of anti-Communism, distilling, analyzing, pleading. October 20, 1956, an editorial, "The Ghosts Are Restless":

> Twenty years ago Communism seemed to reach an ultimate level of the macabre in the mad Purge Trials, with their self-destroying confessions of impossible deeds, and their aftermath of rubber-soled executions in the cellars of the Lubyanka. The Trials, however, sink back to the banal in the wild light of the unwinding process now going on in Eastern Europe.
>
> Seven years ago in Hungary four Communist leaders were put to death and buried in dishonored ground, as "bourgeois nationalists," Titoists, and agents of U.S. intelligence: the then-Foreign Minister, Laszlo Rajk, along with General George Palffy, Dr. Tibor Szoeny, and Andras Szalai. Last week the rotted corpses of these four men were exhumed, exposed in great biers mounted in the center of Budapest, and made ready for reburial in a new cemetery designed as a national pantheon.

The godless anti-religion of Communism is driven to complete the symbolic cycle of its black inversion of true religion. To its myriad rites of crucifixion, it now adds a blasphemous resurrection.

On a single day two hundred thousand Hungarians walked past these biers—not by command in the usual Communist mode, but spontaneously, by individuals and family groups. They were silent, but what was in their hearts? Under totalitarian rule, where so little can be uttered, we must look deep. At the literal level the whole issue was from the mass point of view a senseless dispute between rival sets of jailers. For all the people knew, the exhuming was only an excuse for a new round of killings; with another shift in political line next year, the four corpses might be thrown in a lime pit.

But surely those vast throngs were telling each other and us that it is their buried freedom that they mourn for, and its future resurrection for which they hope and wait.

Two weeks later, those Hungarians on whom James Burnham had his eye did exactly that: they resurrected their freedom. Three weeks later, they were mostly dead, run over by Russian tanks, some of them, others of them hanged or imprisoned.

But the spirit was regenerated, and every month, every year, the writers in *National Review* did what they could to press hope, and to maintain the moral perspective. We are justly proud that one of our readers became the leader of the Free World, who exercised the critical voice in the critical deliberations of the Eighties.

And, on bended knee, we give thanks to Providence for the transfiguration of Russia, thanks from those of us who lived to see it, and thanks to those, departed, who helped us to understand why it was right to struggle to sustain the cause of Western civilization.

—WFB

Four

OUT OF THE DEPTHS, INTO RETIREMENT

October 1991–December 2005

W E WERE INTO the Nineties and looked across the millennial bar. As I mentioned earlier, I had stepped down as hands-on editor-in-chief in 1990. In 2004 I would take a further step into retirement, deeding ownership of the magazine to five trustees. But meanwhile, the swirl went on. I got around to translating and explicating the uses of the Latin cliché (née aphorism) Quod licet Jovi, non licet bovi. It is a maxim I have found useful for decades. The Latin reminds those willing to listen to the argument that the occasional foreign word can have the arresting effect desired, in the struggle to translate human thought into words. Foreign phrases are most useful, in my own experience, in invoking generic principles, as in the use of laissez-faire. ("There we go, laissez-faire one more time" was the derisory denunciation by a British MP opposing one of Mrs. Thatcher's steep tax reductions).

On the matter of linguistic correctness I wrote to the *New York Times* to protest a published criticism of my use of the word "transpire." And we let readers of "Notes & Asides" weigh whether Buckley was using "pompous language," submitting, in one dispute, to the ruling of a totally persuasive lumberyard owner.

Intra-ideological corrections and amplifications were entered. Milton Friedman rebuked co-libertarian Bill Rickenbacker for declining Social Security benefits on the grounds that he had opined against the system ("The United States is in a way a club to which I belong, not indeed voluntarily but by reason of birth. . . . I bear the burdens it imposes. I am equally entitled to receive the benefits").

All very well, but this did not clarify the question whether Art Buchwald could master the idiom of a conservative Republican.

Ever on the question of shadings in language, I considered the matter of interrogatives:

"You're ready to go on to Section 4, yes?"

"You're ready to go on to Section 4, no?"

Which formulation highlights your readiness more acutely?

Whichever—we came to the end of an era. And my closing was pretty expansive, even a little sentimental.

∾

October 21, 1991

Dear Mr. Buckley:

You can't imagine my excitement upon reading, when you visited the *Titanic* in 1989, of your descent two and a half miles into the ocean! If only you hadn't come up.

Sincerely,
Thomas J. Sinsky
Madison, Wisc.

Dear Mr. Sinsky: Did you not know that I was irrepressible? Cordially, WFB

November 4, 1991

Dear Mr. Buckley:

  Recently it was my pleasure and privilege to renew
my subscription. Through this process I acquire a nice
collection of books and lend a little help to your
good effort. However, I found myself wondering when
my subscription did expire. And further, would I live
long enough to enjoy all issues? Do you have any inside
dope? In case I should leave this nice place too soon,
could you forward all remaining issues?

Thank you,
Bill Ivins
Murrieta, Calif.

Dear Mr. Ivins: Where you're headed, NR *is exfoliated daily from angels'
wings. Cordially, WFB*

March 2, 1992

Dear Mr. Buckley:

  Our client, Michael Krafft, a European ship owner,
asked us to relay to you his shock over the recent
decision by a federal district court in St. Louis, Judge
Clyde Cahill presiding, that Mr. Krafft's Miami shipping
company, and his sailing clipper ships, the largest ever
built, may not use the term "clipper" in their names.
Mr. Krafft's company, Star Clippers, Inc., had been sued
by the St. Louis cruise company Clipper Cruise Lines,
Inc., operators of motor-driven, shallow-draft luxury
vessels. Mr. Krafft is very anxious to make known his
bafflement at court action that departs from a tradition
of 150 years . . . everywhere, of the term "clipper."

That term had been coined originally to describe the high-speed sail vessels of the mid nineteenth century.

His ships are based on those designs. One recently has entered cruise service in the Caribbean, the second was launched last fall in Belgium.

Cordially yours,
Alan Bell
Robert Kneeley & Co.
Fort Lauderdale, Fla.

Dear Mr. Bell: Sounds very odd. I can't imagine that the word "clipper" is copyrighted, though odd ownerships abound. Did you know you can't write "bandaid," you have to write "Band-Aid"—because the Johnson Company so to speak owns the name? Copyright laws are very funny and not entirely predictable. When this magazine was preparing to launch, its name was National Weekly. *But the SecState, New York, said: No. That name transgressed on the rights of a journal called* National Liquor Weekly. *We were so disgusted by the whole experience we threw away the "Weekly" and became a fortnightly. Good luck. Cordially, WFB*

August 31, 1992

Memo to: Bill
From: Jim McF.

Maybe you missed this, but if so, a) you should not; and b) you should not deprive our readers of it. The letter is from the *Harvard Lampoon*'s lampoon of our friends at *The Dartmouth Review*, and I have to think they too thought it hilarious. Enjoy:

To the Editor:
Your article last week entitled "Student Democrat's Speech Really Blows" contains several misquotes and

factual errors which I would like to address. First
of all, I did not deliver my speech to "three bored
freshmen and a crippled dog" as you assert, but rather
to a large assembly of people gathered in Freeman
Lecture Hall. You could ask any of those people, and
they would tell you that this is true.

The speech was a rather staid one about the need
for economic reform. At no time in my speech did I
recommend that the government "tax everyone 100 per
cent, but just for a week," or say that we should
"let all of the criminals out of jail for one big,
fun party." I do not agree with these statements, nor
did I say anything even remotely like them.

In the middle of my presentation, I did not leave
to go to the bathroom and not return for 15 minutes.
Neither did I at any point forget what I was talking
about and start to cry. I spoke calmly for 15 minutes
without interruption, after which I answered several
well-put questions.

At no time in my speech did I threaten to kill the
President, nor did I conclude my talk by passing a hat
and "feebly asking for money to buy a sandwich." I
have great respect for the Presidency, and I know full
well that I can eat for free in the dining hall. Your
article was incorrect in reporting all of these facts.
I get the distinct feeling that your reporter was not
even present at my speech.

I would also like to point out to your readers that
my middle name is "Morris" not "Stenchmeister."

Edgar Morris Jones
President
Dartmouth Democrat Club

October 19, 1992

Dear WFB:

  In case you were considering an "Oxymoron of the Decade" contest, don't bother. I have already found the winner. *Newsweek:* June 22, 1992 ". . . Jackson's National Rainbow Coalition brain trust." Wow!

Cordially,
Edward K. Krause
Ann Arbor, Mich.

Dear Mr. Krause: Okay, we transcend our rule against more oxymorons. Cordially, WFB

March 29, 1993

Dear Mr. Buckley:

  At last! After nearly four years of seminary training and two and a half years in parish work, I fortuitously came across the following Biblical maxim: "The wise man's understanding turns him to his right; the fool's understanding turns him to his left" (Eccles. 10:2).
  Now why didn't we learn that in seminary?

Respectfully,
Michael Moore
Oregon City, Ore.

Dear Father Moore: Vatican II decided that such a meaning, imputed to the Left, was sinister. Cordially, WFB

May 10, 1993

Dear Mr. Buckley:

  The enclosed clip, a column by Aissatou Sidime, comes from the *Oakland Tribune,* which relentlessly pushes the liberal agenda--even more so now that it has received a grant from the Gannett Foundation. I draw your attention to the sentence, "As the country moves toward increased ethnic and gender diversity . . ." Increased gender diversity! That's a new one, even for the *Tribune*. Maybe they've been working overtime in the science lab.

Yours truly,
Jim Grodnik
Oakland, Calif.

Dear Mr. Grodnik: Sounds fascinating. On the other hand, I think I've met some of those . . . Cordially, WFB

October 18, 1993

Memo to: Bill
From: Dorothy [McCartney]*

  I think our readers might enjoy seeing the Proust questionnaire *Vanity Fair* printed in its September issue, under the heading: "Can a few simple questions sum up a life? That's the point of the Proust Questionnaire (named for Marcel, who took it twice). *Vanity Fair* updates the notion and tries it out on William F. Buckley Jr."

NR's research director.

What is your idea of perfect happiness? *Heaven*.

What is your greatest fear? *Hell*.

Which living person do you most admire? *Ronald Reagan*.

What is the trait you most deplore in yourself? *My failure to practice the harpsichord more regularly*.

What is the trait you most deplore in others? *Their failure to ask me to play the harpsichord*.

What is your greatest extravagance? *My lifestyle*.

What is your favorite journey? *Going home*.

What do you consider the most overrated virtue? *Introspection*.

On what occasion do you lie? *On many occasions*.

What do you most dislike about your appearance? *My gestating paunch*.

Which living person do you most despise? *Pol Pot*.

Which words or phrases do you most overuse? *"In due course . . ."*

What is your greatest regret? *I read slowly*.

What or who is the greatest love of your life? *J. S. Bach*.

When and where were you happiest? *Age five to seven*.

Which talent would you most like to have? *A retentive and comprehensive memory*.

What is your current state of mind? *Apprehensive*.

If you could change one thing about yourself, what would it be? *I'd like to know how to pray better*.

If you could change one thing about your family, what would it be? *I'd like it to be larger*.

Where would you like to live? *Where I live*.

What do you consider your greatest achievement? *National Review*.

If you could choose how to come back, how would it be? *Stillborn*.

What is your most treasured possession? *My faith*.

What do you regard as the lowest depth of misery?
The loss of faith.

What is your favorite occupation? *The correction of other people's errors.*

What is your most marked characteristic? *Speedwriting.*

What is the quality you most like in a person? *A sense of humor.*

What do you most value in your friends? *Their companionship.*

Who are your favorite writers? *Wilfrid Sheed, John Leonard, Richard Brookhiser, Joe Sobran, D. Keith Mano, Murray Kempton.*

Who is your favorite hero of fiction? *Blackford Oakes.*

Who are your heroes in real life? *The people who overthrew the Soviet Union.*

What are your favorite names? *I haven't any.*

What is it that you most dislike? *Lousy logic, tempestuously waged.*

How would you like to die? *Painlessly.*

What is your motto? *Quod licet Jovi, non licet bovi.*

November 1, 1993

Dear Mr. Buckley:

Why do so many noted conservatives tend to be men of great girth? G. K. Chesterton, Whittaker Chambers, and Rush Limbaugh, for instance. I exclude you from this group, of course. Judging from photos (unretouched, I assume) your waistline hasn't changed in the last forty years.

Robert del Valle
Troy, Mich.

Dear Mr. del Valle: On the last point first, I singled out only last issue that my crowning biological fear is of a gestating paunch. But I'm working on it. If memory serves, most conservative seers have been pleasingly svelte. E.g., Plato, Aristotle, Mark, Matthew, John, Luke, Paul, and Reagan. Cordially, WFB

November 15, 1993

Dear Bill:

  Here is a copy of the letter I sent to our friend
Bill Rickenbacker on the question of accepting
Social Security payments even if you disapprove of
the system.

Cordially,
Milton [Friedman]
Stanford, Calif.

Dear Bill:

  In re your letter to WFB, I use Medicare and every
other service and advantage that is legally available
to me, though like you I oppose Medicare and Social
Security and have for many decades written in favor
of their abolition. I do not believe that there is
any moral conflict involved whatsoever.
  A personal anecdote will perhaps explain best my
justification for that behavior. The Department of
Economics, of which I was a member, voted at one point
to institute an annual prize for the best article
published in its professional journal. As chairman
of the committee to make the final decision for one
year, I requested fellow members of the department to
nominate three articles for the prize. One member of

the department wrote back saying that, since he had
voted against the department's giving the prize, he
felt no obligation to participate in the choice of the
article to receive it. I suspect that as a member of
the department you would have been as outraged as I
was at that reaction.

The United States is in a way a club to which I
belong, not indeed voluntarily but by reason of birth.
However, I have not seceded from it. I bear the
burdens it imposes. I am equally entitled to receive
the benefits. I do not believe that either the one or
the other should inhibit my urging upon the public
the policies that I believe desirable.

Sincerely yours,
Milton Friedman

Dear Mr. Buckley:

I would appreciate a translation of your motto "Quod
licet Jovi, non licet bovi" ("Notes & Asides," Oct. 18).
My sources translate it as "What is permitted to God,
is not allowed to the cow."
I'm sure this is not accurate and will await your
corrections. Thank you very much.

Sincerely,
Mrs. Evelyn Gerety
New Fairfield, Conn.

*Dear Mrs. Gerety: There is no idiomatic sentence that translates Quod licet
Jovi, non licet bovi. But you have hold of the idea: That which God (Jupiter,
Jove) is permitted to do, a cow is not permitted to do. What it boils down to is
an anti-egalitarian aphorism which, very freely translated, would say
something like, "Yes, but you're not Marilyn Monroe." Cordially, WFB*

November 29, 1993

Dear Mr. Buckley:

   I am intrigued by your title on the masthead,
Editor-at-Large. Does this mean that among all
National Review's editors you are the only one let
out of the cage? Or does it mean that you have escaped,
and that those in authority there mean to recapture
you and re-name you Editor-in-Residence?

David Singer
Modesto, Calif.

*Dear Mr. Singer: No one that I know of has offered a reward for my
recapture, and I am not giving myself up. Please do not identify the source of
this letter. Cordially, WFB*

February 7, 1994

Dear Bill:

   I just got my Christmas present from Hertz. It's
the story of the company--beautifully printed and
truly worthwhile. It's the book I always hoped that
somebody would write.

   I don't know if you are on their list or not, but if
you would like to borrow my copy you are in for a
great treat. Hertz is not a company--it's a family,
it's a religion, it's a way of life.

   I assume that you are going to reprint this letter
as you have all my past correspondence. If you do,
would you mention my new book, *Leaving Home*, published

by Putnam's? It's the story of a poor boy who could
never afford a Hertz credit card.

Cheers,
Art [Buchwald]
Washington, D.C.

Dear Art: I am very jealous. I won't read their book. I'll just stick with yours.
Why did you leave home? Cordially, Bill

Mr. Eric Alterman
Washington, D.C.

Dear Eric:

You will perhaps have noticed the excision of your name from the
paperback of the anti-Semitism book, as requested.

Now: Just yesterday I had reason to pick up your book looking for
something on behalf of a friend. I sighed but accepted as inevitable the
populist blather (p. 123) about my superordinate concern for skiers in
Gstaad and yachtsmen in the Caribbean—okay, that's the kind of thing
people qualified to be managing editor of *The Nation* need to say.

But then you referred to me as a "self-styled aristocrat." I would be
grateful if you would explain to me how you came upon that designation.
I have never referred to myself as an "aristocrat," which, incidentally,
aristocrats would never do. Ah! Maybe that's it! Because I have never called
myself an aristocrat, I therefore take on that mannerism of an aristocrat—
becoming one, to be sure self-styled. On the other hand, you mention my
grandfather. I frequently refer to my grandfather, the sheriff of Duval
County in Texas. I say about him that he was renowned for his loyalty to
the Democratic Party and for his emphasis on law and order, but that his
loyalty to the former exceeded his loyalty to the latter, inasmuch as though
he died in 1904, he voted for Lyndon Johnson in 1948.

But anyway, I'd be grateful to hear from you on this point. And you must tell me how I can spot "self-styled" aristocrats all by myself. Share your secrets! Be a redistributionist à outrance.

With cordial regards,
Bill

Dear Mr. Buckley:

Thanks very much for your thoughtful note of December 8. I did not receive it until Christmas Eve, but sat down to answer immediately, even though I imagine you are probably in Gstaad or, better yet, some Caribbean island of which I have not even heard.

I am sincerely sorry to hear that my name has been excised from the paperback of the anti-Semitism book. I rather appreciated your making such extensive use of my arguments re Brother Buchanan, as I believe I said in the opening sentences of my original ill-fated note. I was hoping that the guilt that you truly deserved to experience as a result of the carelessness involved in your errors would at a minimum garner me an invitation on *Firing Line* one evening when my friend Mark Green was busy running for some office somewhere. Alas, it was not to be.

When I was a freshman in college, in 1978, I attended a speech you gave at Bailey Hall on the campus of Cornell University. I recall quite vividly a young man, his voice breaking with emotion, asking you, as he called it, "one simple question: Mr. Buckley," he quivered, "have you ever gone hungry?" Your reply, and I believe I am quoting you accurately though this was nearly 16 years ago, was, "Why, yes, my yacht experienced an unfortunate shortage of stuffed goose recently between Nassau and the Bahamas."

At the time, I remember thinking, "Well, hey," or some such adolescent expression, "this Buckley fellow is playing by different rules than the rest of us." Mr. Buckley, forgive my saying so, but in a nation that has no historic tradition of an aristocratic class, you are clearly an aristocrat. The fact that you never refer to yourself as one is, as you guessed, further proof of your appropriated station. I grew up in Scarsdale, New York. And I can tell you from experience that the vulgar rich among my friends' parents and my parents' friends did not refer to themselves as "the vulgar rich." This hardly made them any less so.

You might have argued--I think it would have been more profitable, actually--that in a nation such as ours, all but invented by a bastard from the West Indies, aristocrats are by definition "self-styled." The modifier in your case was therefore redundant, and hence, also gratuitous. I would grant that point, but surely a victory so slight is beneath the quality of those to which you have become accustomed. I mean, after electing a malleable dolt like Ronald Reagan to the highest office in the land, getting a punk like me to withdraw an adjective must seem an awful anticlimax.

As for how can you, too, recognize aristocrats on the street, this, I fear, is a talent that has either been born to one or has not. Your grandfather, however, seems to me to be quite safe. No aristocrat of any style would have voted for Lyndon Johnson. And on this matter, I must say, I agree with you aristocrats.

With warm regards,
Eric Alterman
Washington, D.C.

Dear Eric:

Nice try. But then your problems are, of course, insuperable. To begin with, your memory is defective: I don't even know what stuffed goose tastes like. And the lilt of the sentence you ascribe to me doesn't fit, unless the context in which it was said was comic; but then that in turn does not fit the image of the student-in-tears.

Your modifiers are once again misplaced in referring to the "malleable" Mr. Reagan. You see, it was not he who proved malleable, but the Soviet Union. Mr. Reagan ordered the Berlin Wall to come down, and it did; he ordered Communism to go to the ashheap of history, and it did. We know that my grandfather's vote for LBJ was done on his behalf, but the Democratic grave-robbers were certainly not self-styled.

And on the other business. 1) If your parents' vulgar rich friends did not so designate themselves, then you'd be wrong in referring to them as "self-styled vulgar rich." 2) That which is redundant is not necessarily gratuitous. 3) The victory I have won may be slight in your eyes, but inasmuch as it is the only victory I set out to win, you will acknowledge that your capitulation on this modest point is welcome.

Yours cordially,
Bill

May 16, 1994

Dear Mr. Buckley:

National Review needs something a little bit more. I don't mean anything more with respect to the commentary, impeccable as it is, but something that would add to *NR*'s personality. The emblems of *Foreign Affairs* (the horseman), *The Atlantic* (Poseidon riding the waves), and *The New Republic* (a galleon on the high seas) give those periodicals a distinguished image.

Perhaps the time has come when *National Review* should adopt its own distinctive badge. Maybe a bust of Edmund Burke with a quill above his head with some Latin, "Annuit coeptis"? Or a phoenix descending from the heavens? An armor-clad crusader atop his charging steed? Think it over.

Respectfully yours,
Chris A. Varones
Orland Park, Ill.

Dear Mr. Varones: I like the idea. Herewith an invitation to everyone to nominate an appropriate ideolographic logo. Cordially, WFB

August 29, 1994

Dear Mr. Buckley:

I received your disappointing letter earlier this week. I am amazed that you believe that the fact that you "routinely" publish the letters written to you obviates the need for the common decency of asking a person's permission before doing so. You have now published letters of mine three times without asking and are obviously too old to change your ways. I will therefore spare you a lecture, and say simply that, Mr. Buckley, you are not, after all, a gentleman. When your number comes up, and your supplicants are fawning over your alleged virtues, as they have done for your racist and anti-Semitic comrade, Richard Nixon, I will do my best to remind the larger public of the truth.
   Please feel free to print this letter.

With all sincerity,
Eric Alterman
Washington, D.C.

Dear Mr. Alterman: If I can be confident that your voice will represent the Opposition, I shall confidently approach the Pearly Gates. Cordially, WFB

November 21, 1994

To the Editor
Washington Post

Sirs:

Michael Lind writes ["Calling All Crackpots: A New Conservative Credo: No Enemies on the Right," Oct. 16] that "not one of today's timid conservative intellectuals has dared to mock [Pat] Robertson, the powerful leader of the Christian Coalition. Wm. F. Buckley Jr., who drove Birch leader Robert Welch from the ranks of the respectable right, has repeatedly defended Robertson, even though the latter's claim that a 'tightly knit cabal' of Satan-worshipping occultists is secretly running the United States through the Council on Foreign Relations makes Bircher conspiracy theories look tame."

Mr. Lind would have done better to proclaim my ignorance than my cowardice. You see, I (along with William Bennett and Midge Decter, also cited by Mr. Lind) have gone no further than to defend many of Pat Robertson's public positions on what ails U.S. policy. Mr. Lind makes it sound as though Mr. Robertson's theory about the Satanists who run U.S. foreign policy were as broadly identified with Robertson as Copernican astronomy is with Galileo. Well, if Pat Robertson indeed believes that crazy stuff, I here and now expel him from the conservative movement, and await a Silver Star for courage from Mr. Lind. To be sure, having flaunted my ignorance, I should make the further admission that I have not personally looked into the recent activities of Satan-worshipping occultists, and should I at some point in the future discover that they are indeed responsible for American foreign policy, a lot of things begin to fall into place, sort of like the centrality of the sun, if you see what I mean.

Yours faithfully,
Wm. F. Buckley Jr.

December 19, 1994

Dear Mr. Buckley:

  Eric Alterman's letter [Aug. 29], berating you for
publishing his letters in "Notes & Asides" without
consent, opened my heretofore blind eyes. It dawns
on me that you haven't published all my letters. Now,
I'm similarly outraged in an antithetical mode when
I devote valuable time to inditing ineffably luminous
epistles and you callously ignore them. Therefore,
I will demand that if you are not going to publish
my literary bijoux you notify me by certified mail
immediately on receipt. If I agree, you will be free
to discard them. That said, I will expect your
abject apology and deferential rejection post-haste,
as directed.

G. P. Lucchetti
Oak Park, Ill.

*Dear Mr. Lucchetti: Herewith my apologies, and earnest money on my
determination to reform. Cordially, WFB*

April 17, 1995

Memo to: WFB
From: Linda [Bridges]*

  Bill, Why don't we publish your obituary of Bill
Rickenbacker in "Notes & Asides"? It would fit nicely
there, with all the quotes from his letters.

---

*Successor to my sister Priscilla as managing editor of *NR*.

Memo to: Linda
From: WFB

Herewith, in loving memory.

William F. Rickenbacker, RIP

Bill Rickenbacker came thirty-five years ago to *National Review* as a senior editor, and life was wonderful in his company. He retreated after ten years or so, went into business for himself, wrote eight books, and continued his studies of music, of languages, and of the canon of Western thought.

But he never lost touch with us and in 1991, with Linda Bridges, published the book *The Art of Persuasion.* A few years ago, responding to a rebuke for his failure to visit New York more often, he wrote me, "I too wish I could move around a bit more, but I seem to have simplified my life a good deal in recent years. Three or four hours a day at the old piano will nail a fellow down good and hard. But I have dreams, dreams in full color, not to mention aroma, of lunch at Paone's [the reference is to the restaurant around the corner on 34th Street and Third Avenue, heavily patronized by *National Review*], which, by the way, why doesn't somebody burn it down and rebuild it up here in God's country?" The formulation of that last sentence is an inside joke, dating back to the opening sentence of an editorial written by the late Willmoore Kendall for *NR*. It began, "Last week at Harriman House, which by the way why doesn't somebody burn it down . . ." There was some concern not over the sentiments expressed but over the diction used, until Bill relieved us by declaring that Kendall had used an anacoluthon, defined as an abrupt change within a sentence to a second construction inconsistent with the first, sometimes used for rhetorical effect; for example: I warned him that if he continues to drink, what will become of him. Bill, in his letter, went on about his schedule. "Now I'm moving steadily through the 15 volumes of the collected utterances and effusions of Edmund Burke, and the more I see of him the less I trust him. He keeps reminding me of Everett Dirksen—not that Dirksen ever reminded me of Burke."

Bill was a professionally qualified pianist. "I've recorded," he wrote me, "to my satisfaction, four short pieces of our great teacher, the Bach of Bachs. Schubert comes next, and then a dollop of Chopin. I find this project far more difficult than it was 25 years ago. Two trends have been in play: my standards have risen, and my physical capacity has fallen. When I piled up my airplane and broke a dozen bones including my right wrist, I didn't advance the cause; my right hand, if I don't pay good attention, is still in danger of being shouted down by the unruly Bolshevik in my left—a faction that gathered its preternatural strength during ten years of intensive club-gripping on the golf course." He had been captain of the golf team at Harvard. And, like his father, Captain Eddie, he flew airplanes, until glaucoma stopped him.

His curiosity was boundless. "Did you see my Unamuno in the current *Modern Age*?" The reference was to an essay he had just published. "Next comes Ortega y Gasset. I've read 21 volumes of his and am now organizing my notes. I'll probably have 60 pages of notes in preparation for an eight-page piece. I don't think the name for that is scholarship; more like idle dithering."

It seemed endless, his curiosity. "I've been studying Hebrew very hard and loving it all the way. A wonderful language. Since college days I've wanted to read the Psalms in Hebrew; now I shall."

He was not altogether a recluse. Last year he consented to address my brother Reid's public-speaking school in South Carolina. Reid asked how should he introduce Bill's speech. Reid sent me a copy of Bill's suggested titles:

—How I Spent My Summer
—What the North Wind Said
—Counselor Said I Couldn't Eat Dinner Till I Wrote Home

—Why I Hate My Sis

—Legalization of Crime: Pros & Cons

—Was Mozart Queer?

—Are Lasers Protected under the Fourth Amendment?

—The Bartender's Guide to the Upstairs Maid

—Merde! Golfing Decorum in Postwar France

—Public Speaking Minus One: A Tape Cassette of Wild but Intermittent Applause, with Stretches of Silence to Be Filled with Remarks by the Apprentice Orator

—Sexual Repression in Emily Dickinson's Punctuation

—Why I Am Running for President (applause)

—Why Dead White Males Don't Laugh

—Do Hydrogen and Oxygen Look like Water? I Ask You!: Chemistry Disrobed and Shown to Be the Fraud It Is

His concern for public affairs was alive as ever. "There has been some talk of flying the flag at half mast," he wrote me, "until the Court's decision [permitting the burning of the flag] is nullified, but I don't think a gesture of mourning is in order when the battle has hardly begun. Instead, I'm flying my own flag at full mast, but upside down, in the international signal of distress. A flag that has been abandoned by its own country is certainly in distress, and I intend to fly mine upside down until the Court turns right side up."

He enjoyed always the exuberant flash of muscle that interrupted, and gave perspective to, his serenity. "I have been a grandfather for five days now and I am growing crotchety. I have told both my boys and both my stepsons that the first one calls me gramps gets a knee in the groin but I doubt if I'll be safe much longer."

That was correct—he wasn't safe much longer. It was last fall that the cancer came. But after the operation, he wrote to soothe me. ". . . my moribundity is no more serious than anyone else's of similar time in grade. The so-called treatment, which is in reality, as I need not tell you, a form of Florentine poisoning, offers the advective cruelty of the absence of wine. Anyway I now have two Sanskrit grammars, a matched pair, and will present one copy to [his doctor] when next I see her, which I fear will be on Monday. My hope is that she with her wise Velázquez-brown eyes will find a way to administer my Sanskrit intravenously, with a dash of curry and the faintest after-aroma of papadams. (Do you remember when our mothers could buy papadams in large flat tins from India, the cakes packed between green tobacco leaves?)"

And, a week later, a letter describing his doctor, whom he much admired. But halfway down the page, "EGGS ON FACE DEPT. When I sent you the copy of her letter, I failed to proofread it with care, and discovered later that when she says she may extend a certain life span by two or three months, she means years. I double-checked her on this. So relax, mon vieux: It will be longer than you think before your life and property shall be safe."

The doctor was right the first time. But Bill went on with his work. "I've been having fun writing my study of three-letter words. Since the emphasis is on their history and not their definition or use, I have elbow room in the definitions. 'Gun' for instance, which has a very peculiar etymology, I define as 'a metallic pipe through which missiles, which have been excited by chemical explosions in their fundaments, are hurled airmail to their recipients.' For the kind of people who like that sort of thing that's the sort of thing those people will like. And although I have made it a rule to exclude proper nouns, I couldn't resist 'Eli,' but I think I shall stay my mighty arm and not tell you how I defined Eli until Nancy [Bill's wife, a painter] is rich and famous."

Bill had for a while been reading religious literature, and now he wrote, "I'm reading the Pope's book. I bought a copy for each of my boys, gave one to Tommy, and held one back to read myself before giving it to Jamie. I should buy a third, because I want the book at my elbow always. It's so drenched in wisdom and experience and devotion that I can't take it in in one reading. I read sentence after sentence two or three times. What a man! Among the great souls of history, I say."

A month later, from Switzerland, I spoke with Nancy on the telephone. She had difficulty in speaking, but told me Bill had been given three or four days more to live. I asked whether I should write to him. Yes she said, giving me the fax number. I had never before written, or spoken, to someone on his deathbed, with whom circumspection was no longer possible. So I wrote to my dear and gifted friend,

"*Wm,* [This was our protocol, dating back three decades: All letters to one another would begin, Wm, and be signed, Wm]

"*This is not the season to be jolly. Miracles do happen, Evelyn Waugh wrote in* National Review, *'but it is presumptuous to anticipate them.' It will happen to us all, I brightly observe, but you should feel first the satisfaction of knowing that soon you will be in God's hand, with perhaps just a taste of Purgatory for the editorial you wrote when Bobby was killed, though I here and now vouchsafe you the indulgence I merited on declining to publish it. Second, the satisfaction of being with that wonderful Nancy in your tribulation; and third, the knowledge that those who have known you count it a singular blessing to have experienced you. I send my prayers, and my eternal affection. Wm*"

In fact he lived three weeks more and, before losing the use of his writing hand, indited his own obituary—two paragraphs of biographical data, and the closing sentences:

"A bug or two showed up last fall and began to do what a bug does best, namely, to make a joke out of life's spruce intentions, and to provide a daily wage or two for journalists, whose business it is not my duty as a Christian to inquire into. Sometime between when this ink and mine go dry the bugs will have had their day . . . He leaves behind him his wife and two devoted sons, two daughters-in-law, three grandchildren, a beloved sister, an unfinished manuscript or two, and a heart filled with blessings. May he rest in peace."

August 14, 1995

Miss Roberta Greene
The Greene Group

Dear Miss Greene:

Given the fact that I don't think I have ever seen a copy of *Folio* magazine, it was slightly startling to see myself pictured in a full-page ad as though it were the first magazine I turn to. And then there was that awful quote up top, which appeared to have been spoken by me. I would rather be shot than use the word "indubitably."

Yours faithfully,
Wm. F. Buckley Jr.

September 11, 1995

Dear Mr. Buckley:

I am a 12-year-old boy from Oyster Bay, New York. If you could give me advice for life, what would it be?

Sincerely,
Kalman Gabriel
Oyster Bay, N.Y.

Dear Kalman: Don't grow up. Cordially, WFB

May 6, 1996

Dear Mr. Buckley:

I sought God for his wisdom and He referred me to you for yours. What is a well-read, red-white-and-blueblooded conservative bachelor to do when he finally falls in love, but with an intractable bleeding-heart liberal? Can love truly conquer all, even ignorance?

Respectfully yours,
Brett M. Decker
Royal Oak, Mich.

Dear Mr. Decker: Well . . . er, just how ignorant? Can she read? Advise. Cordially, WFB

Dear Mr. Buckley:

   It is one of my goals in my personal and professional life is [*you already said is*] to find my name on the inside of *National Review*--I hope as a writer someday [*some day*] for you [*No. A writer "for" somebody is a speech, script, or gag writer.*] and your superior magazine, but for now, I have the intermediate goal of attempting to express myself in your Notes & Asides page. Any editorial help you can give me would be greatly appreciated.

Dear Mr. Buckley:

   I have a way to save America from the continued ravages of liberalism and it is such a brilliant and simple idea, [*no comma*] that I am surprised none of your readers, most of which [*of whom*] for obvious reasons would hold positions of superior intellect and business acumen [*Why should this be obvious? And you do not "hold" a position of superior intellect, nor a position of acumen. Try, Most of whom, I assume, are of superior intellect and business acumen*], had not suggested it earlier [*had suggested it earlier*] through this venue.

We have each current subscribing member of the
National Review [*Let each subscriber to* National
Review] not just submit to you a prepaid subscription
of *National Review* as a gift for a friend [*not only
send in a prepaid subscription to* National Review *as a
gift for a friend*]--as your superb magazine rightfully
[*rightly*] often advertises [*often urges us to do*]--but
we make sure we send the gift subscription to our most
liberal of friend(s) [*but we send a gift subscription
to our most liberal friend(s)*]. The eloquence and
power of the intellectual arguments within each
subscription of *National Review* [*within each issue
of* National Review] could not help but penetrate
the thickest of liberal mindsets [*could not help
penetrating even the thickest of liberal mindsets*].

Respectfully yours,
Robert W. Freniere
South Hadley, Mass.

*Dear Mr. Freniere: That's a terrific idea. And glad to help on the diction.
Keep it up! Cordially, WFB*

May 20, 1996

Dear Chairman Bill:

   I notice with distinct pleasure that, every
time I find *National Review* correspondence in my
mailbox, it has been violently wadded up. Not the
usual carelessness we've learned to expect from
mail handlers, mind you, but the malevolent,
purposeful act of some Postal Service gnome driven
to apoplexy by the mere sight of an envelope with
an *NR* return address.

I first discovered this phenomenon in 1967 at the University of Oregon, where I learned that I could actually induce a sort of frothing at the mouth on the part of budding campus liberals by simply switching a nearby television to *Firing Line* and turning the volume knob clockwise. Sometimes, it's the little things that foster joy of living.

Your Friend and Ally,
Glenn D. Baker
Ashford, Wash.

Dear Mr. Baker: Yes indeed, it is the little things. You do make it a point, do you not, of affixing postage stamps commemorating pestilential figures in our history upside down? Very important. It helps, too, to affect deafness when Internal Revenue rings. Cordially, WFB

May 23, 1996

Bill Buckley:

I have wanted to tell you this for years: You are the second worst-dressed s.o.b. on television.

Cordially,
Harold Fliner
Madison, Tenn.

Dear Mr. Fliner: Who's ahead of me? Cordially, WFB

July 11, 1996

WFB: Actually, no one. You are tops. I classified you as No. 2 only because I felt it'd improve the odds of eliciting a reaction from you--and it worked.
Cordially, Harold Fliner

Dear Mr. Fliner: Who's the worst-dressed non-s.o.b.? Cordially, WFB

February 24, 1997

Numero Uno--

   Having read your column on Gingrich, I am minded to
ask, What in the hell is a regularly scheduled
tricoteuse? Or an irregularly scheduled tricoteuse?
   Oh, Bill . . .

Blessings upon you,
Numero Dos [James Jackson Kilpatrick]
Charleston, S.C.

Dear Sir: Miss Carlson appears on Capital Gang *every other week. That
makes her "regularly scheduled," correct? She takes vapulatory pleasure from
the pain & torment caused to the bourgeoisie, which makes her—in the word
used by Charles Dickens to describe the sadists who surrounded the
guillotine and clucked out their pleasure as they did their knitting—a
tricoteuse. Right? Advise. Cordially, #2*

Dear Bill:

   Concerning my endorsement of Samuel Tanenhaus's
book *Whittaker Chambers*, you should not be in any
doubt: the research and writing are excellent, but
I was particularly enchanted by the discovery that
Chambers was a voice on behalf of *The Affluent Society*
and other Galbraith writing in the editorial precincts
of *National Review*. How good he was in his advanced
years! I take it from your letter that I should close
down on endorsements for a while. I had thought
of giving you an endorsement for your recent book,
Buckley: The Right Word. It would have been,

"Everybody knows that William Buckley is a master of words; it is only the use to which he puts them that restrains one's enthusiasm."

Yours faithfully,
Ken [John Kenneth Galbraith]
Cambridge, Mass.

Dear Ken: No riposte. On this one, you win. A deep bow. Ever, Bill

May 19, 1997

Dear Bill:

   After nearly nine years on the Hill, I thought I had, at one time or the other, read or heard the most ridiculous comments ever uttered. (You need only spend one hour with the *Congressional Record*.)
   But I think I've found one that gets the yearly prize. On the eve of the House vote on "family planning" the president of the Audubon Society weighed in.
   In his letter to members of Congress, Audubon President John Flicker declared, "National Audubon Society wishes to remind you that we approach population growth as one of the most critical environmental issues threatening the survival of birds and their habitat."
   Pretty good, eh?

Warmly,
Tim [Goeglein]
Washington, D.C.

Dear Tim: Yes, pretty good; pretty awful. Cordially, WFB

July 28, 1997

Dear Mr. Buckley:

 On a recent flight, a stewardess offered me a
selection from an all too bland stack of magazines.
I triumphantly pulled out my *NR* and began to read.
Upon deplaning, I realized I'd left it in the seat
pocket in front of me. At first, I worried my collection
would be short. Then it occurred to me that maybe my
loss could be another's gain. Since I fly about as
often as you publish, I've decided to turn this mishap
into practice, with the hope that my small gesture
may enlighten the lives of others. Just think, if
everyone . . .

Only my best,
Maury Kauffman
Nutley, N.J.

*Dear Mr. Kauffman: A terrific idea! But don't leave one in the cockpit. The
pilot would insist on finishing it before landing, and we don't want the public
to be inconvenienced. Cordially, WFB*

August 11, 1997

Dear Mr. Buckley:

 Having just received my *National Review* Gold
MasterCard, I hereby await permission to begin
charging to my heart's delight.

Sincerely,
Edward Loss Jr.
College Park, Md.

Dear Mr. Loss: Having acquired a National Review MasterCard, you should declare in favor of private deficit spending, while of course maintaining our collegial position against federal deficit spending. Cordially, WFB

September 1, 1997

Mr. Ronald W. Allen
President, Delta Airlines
Atlanta, Ga. 30320

Dear Mr. Allen:

On Wednesday, June 12, I traveled Delta to Atlanta (from LaGuardia) at 1 P.M. The lunch (roast-turkey sandwich) was okay. After a long afternoon I raced to the airport and took your #524 back to LaGuardia. I was astonished on being told by the flight attendant that we would be served, to eat—pretzels.

I was traveling First Class, but assume my complaint is no different from what it would have been if I had been traveling Economy. In order to get an 8:30 P.M. flight in Atlanta you will want to check in at, say, 7:45. In order to do that, you must leave downtown Atlanta at, oh, 7:10. In order to have had dinner by 7:10 you would need to schedule it for 6 P.M. Most people who fly don't eat at 6 P.M. (Even if they did, what is the harm in offering them a sandwich at 9?)

I wrote a note to the captain, protesting Delta's policy. He agreed wholly with my criticism and urged that I write to management, which I am now doing. It is surely a foolish and self-defeating economy to deny any nourishment to your clients on a two-hour flight beginning at 8:30 P.M. If you persist in these policies, I'd advise you to mount a big sign outside the ticket window: DELTA DOES NOT PROVIDE FOOD. BRING YOUR OWN. The airport is crowded with fast-food stations, and it would have been very easy for the passengers to have brought along something to go with the pretzel. An alternative would be to get

a student to hawk peanut-butter crackers. Maybe Delta could extract
a royalty.

Yours faithfully,
Wm. F. Buckley Jr.

(Mr. Allen was discharged as president of Delta after the arrival of this letter.)

Dear Mr. Buckley:

  Somewhere, someone must have given you the mistaken
notion that you are immune from the rules of civil
discourse. On television tonight, you resorted to the
gratuitous and degrading label "eco-freaks" in a thinly
disguised attempt to win an ecology debate by slander.
Only a "ghoulish freak" would be so devious as to make
so despicable a verbal attack on people who attempt
with good intent to protect our environment (no matter
how effectively or ineffectively they do it).
  Your attitude is that of a pompous, self-centered
reprobate; you consistently obfuscate the issue;
you appear to have the intellect, character, and
communication abilities of pond scum. Your tactics
are matched in freakishness only by your snake-ish
leer and ugly watery-eyed, hawk-nosed countenance.
If these truths hurt, recognize them for what they
are--ad-hominum attacks as degrading, destructive,
and pointless as yours.

O. Oymaa
Odelot, Ohio

Dear Mr. Oymaa: But what do we do with the language at our disposal? A
"freak," as here used, suggests someone lacking in discrimination; thus, e.g.,

vegetable freak, sun freak, salt freak. To use those terms is not to disdain vegetables, the sun, or salt. The question to consider is whether the person or persons I was talking about are in fact indiscriminately concerned with ecology—e.g., Better one spotted owl survive than a mighty river be contained!—in which case you should correct me specifically. And while looking into the matter, take time to familiarize yourself with the spelling of ad hominem, before you misuse it again and run the risk of being dismissed as an abuse freak. Cordially, WFB

March 23, 1998

Dear Mr. Buckley:

The *Boston Globe* published your column on creationism this week and I was shocked--shocked!-- that you had Juliet say, according to the typing monkey, ". . . wherefore art thou, Romeo?"

Did you mean that the monkey still wouldn't get it right? For what Juliet says is: ". . . wherefore art thou Romeo?" She isn't asking why he exists (nor, as some seem to think, is "wherefore" a fancy Elizabethan word for "where") but, in modern parlance, "What did you have to go and be Romeo for?" It's names-- especially Montague and Capulet, of course--that are the issue.

To adapt another line from the play: What's in a comma? Sometimes quite a lot.

Yours severely,
Eva Moseley
Cambridge, Mass.

Dear Mrs. Moseley: Quite right, and nicely corrected. Cordially, WFB

January 25, 1999

Dear Mr. Buckley:

  Two longtime readers of yours are locked in a
longtime dispute it appears only you may be able to
resolve, given your authority in the area concerned.

  One of my closest friends is married to a very
competitive Scrabble player. Unfortunately, the
concept of "friendly competition" is lost shortly
after she draws her first set of tiles. She told me how
she ruined a friendship over a game. It seems her
opponent played "whiter" for big points, prompting her
to protest. How could there possibly be a word like
"whiter" when white is the absence of color? He found
the word in the Scrabble dictionary, and they resumed
play, though she refused to drop the matter of the
inappropriateness of the word "whiter." Shortly after,
she played "jader." Her opponent challenged, and the
word was not found in the Scrabble dictionary. She
argued that if "whiter" was a word, surely "jader"
was. He asked her to use it in a sentence, "The dress
was jader than the last one she tried on." He refused
to let her play the word, and in anger she threw the
board at him. He stormed out of the room. He sent her a
present a couple of weeks later with a note: "You were
right, I was wrong," She opened the wrapping to find a
new Scrabble dictionary. Opening the book to "J," she
found handwritten in blue ink, "jader: a word commonly
used to cheat at Scrabble." The two have rarely spoken
since. In the interest of harmony among conservatives
who happen to be avid Scrabble players, I'm asking
you to adjudicate:

  1. Is "whiter" a word?
  2. Is "jader" a word?

3. Do I dare play Scrabble with either person? Should
I have a lawyer or a psychiatrist present?

Sincerely,
James M. D. Wigderson
Franklin, Wis.

Dear Mr. Wigderson: You have very combative friends! And they are ingenious in the ways of retaliation. But inasmuch as, in this situation, the buck stops here, herewith my finding:

Yes on whiter. Adj. white, whiter, whitest.

No on jader, jade being N. a mineral, most often greenish in color. A lot of nouns can be used as adjectives, but don't let themselves go into the comparative and superlative. "His kangaroo posture made him fragile"— okay; but not, "His posture was kangarooer than Jim's." Cordially, WFB

February 22, 1999

Dear Mr. Buckley:

   The English language can lead to many
misinterpretations, as you have frequently noted.
As our vocabulary expands, increasing the size
of the dictionary, it is no wonder that people do
not understand one another, leading to conflict. An
example of misinterpretation can be found in labeling
food fat free. Do they mean there is no charge for
its fat content or that there is no fat in the product?
Please interpret.

Sincerely,
William M. Fuchs, M.D.
Huntington, N.Y.

Dear Dr. Fuchs: Why should a larger vocabulary cause confusion? It can be, and is, the case that the number of unfamiliar words increases, which is something else. One assumes that doctors of medicine are familiar with the necessary increase in medical terms, which doesn't mean, does it, that you would prescribe for hernia the same medicine as for poison ivy? In re fat free, the ambiguity would disappear if it were properly written—fat-free, a compound adjective. Cordially, WFB

April 5, 1999

Dear Editors:

Please beg, cajole, entice, or simply do whatever works to get Mr. Buckley to run against Hillary. Thank you.

John G. McCarthy
Traverse City, Mich.

Dear Mr. McCarthy: Okay. Will you supply an appropriate intern? Cordially, WFB

Dear Bill:

In a dark world, please, a chink of light! In 2000 Hillary will become a U.S. senator. By 2004--2008 at the latest--she will be president. Question: Is Bill Clinton then to be titled First Gentleman? Well, stranger things have happened . . . or have they?
One to ponder, over the mercies of a double scotch.

Sincerely,
Robert H. Smith, Capt. USN (Ret.)
Reston, Va.

Dear Bob: Yes, that would do a lot for the liquor business, maybe even for the drug business, maybe even for the anesthesia business. Cordially, Bill

May 17, 1999

Dear Mr. Buckley:

  I write in reference to your demanding an intern
in exchange for running against Hillary Clinton to
replace Sen. Moynihan. I fervently hope that thousands
of comely women have now offered their services. But on
the almost unimaginable chance that there has not been a
single female candidate, then for the sake of our United
States, I volunteer myself to serve as your personal
love toy, if you will please oppose Ms. Rodham.

  I know that you'll want to know what I look like, so
my photo is enclosed. I'm in the single-stripe shirt.
The man holding the rugby ball is my dear zaydeh Nyman,
of blessed memory. I'm really very bitter about your
forcing me into this position. I had always hoped, were
I ever to know physical intimacy, that it would be with
a woman. In contrast to some I could name, however, I
value America far more than my own carnal preferences.
To this end, I'm trying to imagine something I would
not do to keep that Medusa out of the U.S. Senate. I
envy Nathan Hale. He only had to give his life.

Reluctantly yours,
Roger P. Glass
Falls Church, Va.

*Dear Mr. Glass: I'll tell you what: I'll give you up as intern, but your
assignment will be to seduce the opposition. Okay? Cordially, WFB*

June 28, 1999

Dear Mr. Buckley:

  What ever happened to the practice of referring to
countries as "she" rather than "it"? In abandoning

this practice, we lose a tremendous richness and
poetry in our language.

   Perhaps *NR* could lead the way in restoring the
use of "she" and "her" rather than "it."

Yours,
Christopher Blunt
Chatsworth, Calif.

*Dear Mr. Blunt: "Spain Declares War on France." Gentleman at club,
newspaper in hand, turns to other gentleman at club: "Why would she want
to do that to her?" . . . I think not. Cordially, WFB*

July 12, 1999

Dear Mr. Buckley:

   I'd like to prevail on your sense of accuracy
and fairness and ask you to consider replacing your
use of the term "Congressman" with "Congressperson."
As I know you are aware, we have people of both
genders in Congress these days, and it is disturbing
and offensive to see a term used that excludes a
significant portion of the House's representation.

Ellen P. Ward
Falls Church, Va.

*Dear Ms. Ward: Forgive me for omitting the six paragraphs that followed
your first, here reproduced. But the arguments you use are very familiar
and we plead nothing more than the clumsiness of the "person" suffix, an
affront to the ear and the plague of freshpersons in college everywhere. Why
not just relax on the subject inasmuch as everything else (quite properly)
is going in the direction of a full acknowledgment of women's rights?
Cordially, WFB*

August 30, 1999

Dear Mr. Buckley:

Something just dawned on me about the Monica Lewinsky scandal: How can we believe the Starr report? Didn't Hillary ban the use of all tobacco products in the White House long before Monica appeared on the scene?

Sincerely,
Joseph B. Matarazzo
Tobyhanna, Pa.

Dear Mr. Matarazzo: You just can't keep people from smoking, I've always maintained. —WFB

October 11, 1999

Dear Mr. Buckley:

Ms. Ellen P. Ward's letter to you regarding the use of "Congressperson" when referring to a member of Congress does not go far enough. Since the last syllable (son) refers to the male gender, the politically correct term of address for a female member of Congress is "Congressperdaughter." This, then, brings into question the use of "female" to refer to a member of the feminine sex. Again, the politically correct term should be "feperdaughter" (God created them male and feperdaughter). This gives rise to other absurdities, such as "woperdaughter" for "woman," "huperdaughterity" for "humanity," "woperdaughteracles" for handcuffs used on "feperdaughters." It then makes a work written by a "woperdaughter," a "woperdaughteruscript." I'm sure that I need not belabor the point.

Sincerely,
William F. Brna
Monongahela, Pa.

September 11, 2000

Dear Mr. Buckley:

I have a small gift that I would like to share with you. I thought of this some 35-40 years ago when I was an undergraduate at Cornell and first became acquainted with your writings. As I hit 60 recently, I figure I'd better do this now, or run the risk that my own mortality (not to mention yours) will otherwise bury my gift with me. While in no way wishing for your demise, I believe I've found the perfect epitaph for you. If you like it, please feel free to use it. I pride myself on its double and triple entendres. It would read, quite simply:

> WILLIAM F. BUCKLEY JR.
> 1925-20XX
> HE WAS ALWAYS RIGHT
> BUT NOW HE'S LEFT

Sincerely,
Michael L. Lichtig, M.D.
Tinton Falls, N.J.

Dear Dr. Lichtig: No no no! When I leave, I'll go right home! Cordially, WFB

January 22, 2001

Dear Mr. Buckley:

After reading your bias-laden post-election column, it becomes more than obvious to me that you should reconsider your strategy concerning sleeping pills. Please consume the entire bottle.

Sincerely,
Stan Strain
Modesto, Calif.

Dear Mr. Strain: If I weren't so sleepy, I'd think you were saying something unfriendly! Cordially, WFB

December 31, 2001

Dear Mr. Buckley:

My mother and I have a difference of opinion on a number of usages and pronunciations. I think someone leans "toward" something, not "towards" it. She thinks "Ree-gan" was the last great president, whereas I insist his name is pronounced "Ray-gun." She believes the *t* in the word "often" is silent; I think it is pronounced. Please settle this so that we may enjoy a peaceful holiday season.

Chauncey Hitchcock
Shelby Township, Mich.

Dear Mr. Hitchcock: Me, I lean toward Raygun, often. Cordially, WFB

June 3, 2002

Dear Bill:

  I delighted in your long ago letter [enclosed] about
velleity. I've never in my life put that horse in
harness, and you were hitching it to an incomprehensible
sentence 22 years ago! These days, like Good Old Joe,
I have a twitchy moribund velleity to get out of bed in
the morning, i.e., a desire unconsummated because of
insufficient resolution.

  Do you limit collision to the meeting of two *moving*
bodies? The authorities appear to be divided, but as
always, your word is final.

Affectionately,
Kilpo [James Jackson Kilpatrick]
Washington, D.C.

*Dear Kilpo: I'm in Switzerland, without the appurtenances I have in
Stamford, so I can only comment from my sense of the word. But surely it
requires two parties in travel? I will stick it in "Notes & Asides" and maybe
come through with something more thoughtful. Affectionately, Bill*

[Enclosed:]
To the Editor [*New York Times*, Feb. 14, 1980]:

  I am aware that you do not publish on your editorial page complaints
from victims of your book reviews, save on the exceptional occasion
when there is grave factual error. I plead that exception in replying to
Anatole Broyard's review of *Who's on First*, in your issue of Feb. 6.

  Permit me to interrupt my complaint just long enough to profess my
admiration for Mr. Broyard and my gratitude for the seriousness with
which he analyzed my book, reaching conclusions that gave me great
satisfaction. I recoil only at his suggestion that I used certain words
incorrectly or ineptly. Now, no one wishes the *New York Times* to become

an organ of verbal disinformation, and so, to dispose of Mr. Broyard's quarrel with my word "velleity," I quote the context in which it was used: "Ambassador Yevgeny Silin, an old-timer, had been en route to Moscow the very day Stalin died—because it had been Stalin's twitchy moribund velleity to liquidate Silin"—i.e., a desire unconsummated because of insufficient resolution. The word could not have been more accurately not to say exquisitely used since its coinage.

Concerning the word "transpire," I disclose a secret. I used to misuse the word, until I read an essay published in *Saturday Review* by Ben Ray Redman in which he pointed to three or four words most regularly misused in English, and one of these was "transpire." That was in 1950, while I was still an undergraduate, and since that time I'd as likely misuse the word "transpire" as the Bureau of Standards would tell you that a kilo weighs 32 feet per second squared.

Your readers should know that the difference between usage and abusage is safely defined as the correspondence between the way in which I use a word, and the way others use it, supposing an unfortunate disparity.

Wm. F. Buckley Jr.
New York, N.Y.

Kilpo: Hang tight on collision. xB

February 24, 2003

Dear Bill:

   I know you are going to be surprised to get a letter from me. I am not asking you for money or a free subscription to *National Review*, which I can pick up for free at LaGuardia Airport when taking the shuttle. Bear with me. I received a letter offering me a free trip anywhere on the *Sea Mariner*, which was going on a world cruise.

I said I wanted to go to Tahiti, and they said, "Bill Buckley has that leg tied up." A month later I got a call: "Do you still want to go to Tahiti?" I said, "Did Buckley fink out on you?"

"Something like that. But since you have similar names, they will think Buckley was you, and vice versa." So I took the offer, and they sent me the brochure for the suites, which cost anywhere from $175,000 to $90,000 for people on welfare.

It suddenly dawned on me that most or all of the passengers who could afford such a cruise would be conservative Republicans, and that is why you were the *Mariner*'s first choice.

Now my question is, if I am you then I have to pretend I am on the right. Or should I admit that I am flying under false colors and am really a bleeding-heart liberal?

If I don't give Trent Lott the benefit of the doubt and say that I don't want to go to war unilaterally with Iraq, will the irate voyagers throw me into the sea?

So I am writing to you for guidance. How do you think I should I play it? Bob Novak said he would tutor me in right-wing language, but I told him you were my mentor.

Art [Buchwald]
Washington, D.C.

Dear Art:

That's not easy to do. You have to get it just right, or the ship will veer off course and take you to the South Pole. We give quick courses at National Review, *and you'll sound like Goldwater (1 hour), Reagan (2 hours), or Milton Friedman (3 hours).*

Remember to have the latest copy of National Review *in your pocket when you walk out of your suite.* NR *is buoyant, so if they toss you overboard, you will float. Have a great sail, and tell them to send the difficult questions to us.*

Ever your obliging mentor,
Bill

May 3, 2004

.Dear Bill:

   No gifts from Craig Koch at Hertz this year. He found out that I am anti-Bush. The only way he could have known is if someone told him. I hope it wasn't you.

Cheers,
Art [Buchwald]
Washington, D.C.

Dear Art: Well, he wrote to me at some length. Beginning soon, Hertz will refuse to rent cars to anybody who is anti-Bush. But you can always ride with me, Art. Ever, Bill

June 14, 2004

Dear Mr. Buckley:

   While taking a practice Graduate Record Examination through the Princeton Review, I came across the following fill-in-the-blank, which I think you might enjoy: "In effect, Buckley's use of such pompous language, rather than adding to the force of his arguments, merely makes one suspect that behind the [blank] verbal façade stands a flimsy supporting architecture." Answer choices:

(A) impressive, (B) brisk, (C) embellished, (D)
crumbling, (E) slouching. The decision here between
A and C is challenging. I picked A and got it wrong.
Is my academic career over?

Best regards,
Patrick Truxes
Los Angeles, Calif.

Dear Mr. Truxes: I'd have thought D would have revealed inside knowledge!
Cordially, WFB

July 12, 2004

Dear Mr. Buckley:

   Though I run a lumberyard in the deep South and
thus am no grammarian, I nearly shot scalding coffee
out of my nose this morning when I read in "The
Week" (May 3) that: "There, but for the grace of God,
went us."
   Are you not perhaps spending too much time off
skiing? Just a ways down this slope you crash headlong
into the dreaded: "There, but for the grace of God,
go me." No? If I am wrong, please don't print this.
I would never live it down at work.

Humbly,
Len Price
Evergreen, Ala.

Dear Mr. Price:

   I like a lot that you are cocksure about things, acknowledging only the
remote possibility that you err!

Do you? No, you're quite right about "we," although it wasn't because I was off skiing. But there are interesting things here, so let us go parsing together: "There, but for the grace of God, went us." "Went us" is a short form for "would we have gone" (to our deaths). G (God) plus A (us) gets us safe conduct in this terrorist clash.

"There will go some of us" is saying that A minus G involves us mortally in the next terrorist clash.

Now, Mr. Price, do you suppose the conditional burden ("but for") threw off the grammatical sense in this construction? I'm not sure, though I don't have Alpine air refreshing my sensibilities right now; which, with the grace of God, I'll have next winter, and will pass on afterthoughts, if there are any.

Cordially,
WFB

December 13, 2004

Dear Mr. Buckley:

A question has bothered me for years. Recently, to find an answer, I consulted *Britannica* (1945) under the headings "time" and "calendar" and came up short. The question: In the designations B.C. and A.D., why is the first in English and the second in Latin?

All good wishes,
Anthony Carroll
Garden City, N.Y.

Dear Mr. Carroll: Well, here's the story. For quite a while they used "P.C."— Pre Christo. But somebody in the Colosseum took a stand against it, shouting out ("clamavit fortiter") that P.C. was too PC to bandy about, whereupon Averroes led the movement to change it to B.C. He was thought neutral in the matter, since he was of course a Muslim. Cordially, WFB

January 31, 2005

> Memo to: WFB
> From: Linda [Bridges]
>
> Dear Bill:
>
> Did you see this? The following is supposedly an
> actual question given on a University of Washington
> physics midterm. The answer by one student struck the
> professor as worth sharing, which is why we now have
> the pleasure of enjoying it:
>
> Bonus Question: Is Hell exothermic (gives off heat)
> or endothermic (absorbs heat)?
> Most of the students wrote proofs of their beliefs
> using Boyle's Law (gas cools when it expands and heats
> when it is compressed) or some variant. One student,
> however, wrote the following:
> First, we need to know how the mass of Hell is
> changing in time. So we need to know the rate at which
> souls are moving into Hell and the rate at which they
> are leaving. I think that we can safely assume that
> once a soul gets to Hell, it will not leave. Therefore,
> no souls are leaving.
> As for how many souls are entering Hell, let's look
> at the different religions that exist in the world
> today. Most of these religions state that if you are
> not a member of their religion, you will go to Hell.
> Since there is more than one of these religions and
> since people do not belong to more than one religion,
> we can project that all souls go to Hell.
> With birth and death rates as they are, we can expect
> the number of souls in Hell to increase exponentially.
> Now, we look at the rate of change of the volume in
> Hell, because Boyle's Law states that in order for

the temperature and pressure in Hell to stay the same, the volume of Hell has to expand proportionately as souls are added.

This gives two possibilities:

1. If Hell is expanding at a slower rate than the rate at which souls enter Hell, then the temperature and pressure in Hell will increase until all Hell breaks loose.
2. If Hell is expanding at a rate faster than the increase of souls in Hell, then the temperature and pressure will drop until Hell freezes over.

So which is it?

If we accept the postulate given to me by Teresa during my freshman year that "it will be a cold day in Hell before I sleep with you," and take into account the fact that I slept with her last night, then Number 2 must be true, and thus I am sure that Hell is exothermic and has already frozen over.

The corollary of this theory is that since Hell has frozen over, it follows that it is not accepting any more souls and is therefore extinct . . . leaving only Heaven, thereby proving the existence of a divine being, which explains why, last night, Teresa kept shouting, "Oh my God!"

This student received the only "A."

July 4, 2005

Dear Mr. Buckley:

What do you make of this from *The New Yorker* (May 2): "For the people waiting outside it, in a line to view Pope John Paul II's body which stretched for more than

three miles, the arms of Bernini's great flanking
colonnades were ahead . . . "

Cordially,
Sayre Miller
Clovis, Calif.

Dear Mr. Miller: I take that to be The New Yorker's *idea of the post-obitum indulgence of the late Holy Father. Cordially, WFB*

August 29, 2005

Dear Mr. Buckley:

I recently had the pleasure of meeting John Thomson
while he was in Kabul collecting material for a
forthcoming article on Afghanistan. John mentioned that
he has enjoyed a long association with *National Review*,
and I asked if he might kindly consider passing along my
offer to you to become a member of the Kabul Yacht Club.

The Kabul Yacht Club can best be described as a
"virtual" yacht club owing to a lack of boats,
facilities, and conditions in Kabul (this, as you
know, is a land-locked country just overcoming the
effects of a seven-year drought). What we do have is
about 200 enthusiastic members, including leading
Afghans, foreign diplomats posted in Kabul, and
Washington leaders such as Secretaries Rumsfeld,
Hoffman, Dobriansky, and Lash. Lt. Gen. Karl
Eikenberry, the new commander of Combined Forces in
Afghanistan, is our newest member.

There are no dues, no obligations, and, frankly, no
standards . . . but there are great friendships and a
truly unique bond among our members.

I hope you will accept the accompanying membership certificate in the Kabul Yacht Club. We'd be honored to include you among our distinguished members. I'm also a member of the New York Yacht Club, and I assure you this is reputable in all respects.

With best regards,
Commodore Mitchell Shivers
Kabul, Afghanistan

Dear Commodore: Okay, fine. You may not be aware that I was covertly ambassador to Afghanistan during the Reagan administration. I don't have a boat any more, but perhaps when I come over you can lay one on? Yours faithfully, WFB

Mr. Buckley:

  While growing up in the Midwest I don't remember ever encountering a grammatical construction such as: "Your imagination should be able to handle that, no?"
  Why not end with "yes"? And what response indicates agreement or disagreement when the query ends in "no"?
  Your erudite clarification would be appreciated.

Sincerely,
Steven L. Wentworth
Yardley, Pa.

Dear Mr. Wentworth: Very interesting. As in other matters in language, doing what comes naturally tends to be the thing to do. The negative is obviously called for in French ("Tu désires du café, non?") and Spanish ("¿Tomas café, no?"). If one were to expand the negative locution here, we'd have "You're going to have coffee, aren't you?" And there is the negative, poking its head up. Aren't you? . . . Are you not? The sentence you quote is constructed to suggest that the addressee's imagination is (presumably) sufficient to cope with the problem; so that the indicated answer if the imagination were insufficient would be: No. A "yes" could be accomplished by a nod of the head, or—silence. Cordially, WFB

December 5, 2005

Dear Mr. Buckley:

   In forming my impression of the unrest among our allies in France, I am forced to ask: Is there a Gallic equivalent of the German term "Schadenfreude"?

Regards,
John P. Glynn
Chicago, Ill.

Dear Mr. Glynn: Yes. It's "joie de vivre." Cordially, WFB

December 31, 2005

To: Beloved readers, friends
Re: "Notes & Asides"

I regretfully conclude that "Notes & Asides" can't continue as a regular feature of National Review. *The reason is: We aren't getting enough letters that qualify as "N&A" material—inquisitive, zany, confused, annoyed, piquant. The feature has had a very good run, nearly 40 years, and has also served as repository for my own material—speeches, obituaries, journal entries. But we won't close down the column; merely run it when there is material at hand. We trust you will be disappointed, and we thank you for all that you have done over so many years to maintain its lively life. We close the regular feature with, appropriately, my farewell appearance—at my 80th-birthday party at the Pierre Hotel in New York, on November 17:*

Ladies and gentlemen, Christo [Buckley], Bill Rusher, Jeff Hart:

About ten years ago, a thoughtful group of people convened in my honor at the behest of the Museum of Radio and Television. Their tribute was extensive and generous. Then, at the end of an evening already long, my turn came. What I did was point my finger at the participating principals, who were Mike Wallace and George Plimpton, Taki Theodoracopulos and Bill vanden Heuvel, Bob Batscha and my son, Christopher; and then at the crowded but wilting dining room. I said that the only way I could hope to compensate their kindness would be to decline so much as to enumerate the *names* of those to whom I owed thanks, let alone describe their contributions. The alternative—to single out everyone who had had a hand in the event—would have made for an even longer evening.

It actually crossed my mind to try the same dodge here tonight, with you. But I didn't have the nerve. At my age, you can't get away with youthful unseemliness, let alone trip lightly over profound indebtedness. Perhaps, before leaving the scene finally, I should compose a doxology, useful on public occasions, recitable at the close of ceremonies, and no less sincere for having been written out, like the Lord's Prayer.

If I had undertaken to write out doxological expressions of praise and gratitude, the requirements of brevity—one can, after all, go on for just so long—would have exercised a useful disciplinary effect. One thinks of limitations placed even on the number of the original disciples. And even there, one of their number turned out to be a security risk. I doubt that Bill vanden Heuvel would happily be reminded of his remarks about me and my work made ten years ago. Certainly he would not want to repeat his testimonial if there was any possibility that his daughter would overhear him. She is, of course, the publisher of *The Nation* magazine, which last week announced that for the first time in 147 years, it was generating a profit!

Talk about security risks! The single journal of opinion in all of America which is running a profit is the staunch socialist weekly—whose publisher emeritus every now and then reaffirms his faith in the innocence of

Alger Hiss. Maybe if Ed Capano went public with his secret belief in the innocence of Sacco and Vanzetti, that disclosure would have a magical effect on *National Review*'s balance sheet. Alternatively, he could take lessons in socialist economic management.

I am glad I touched on the subject of publishing economics because that induces a moment's reflection on two sets of people.

The first set are most of them dead. They are the 50 or 60 people who stepped forward—I have to admit, after a fair amount of coaxing and even a little firebrand persuasion—to underwrite the appearance of the first issue of *National Review* 50 years ago. My two-year personal money-raising campaign included seven meetings at the home of Morrie Ryskind, the great humorist and furtive conservative thundercloud in Hollywood, transformed into equity salesman for National Review, Incorporated. Those two years brought in pledges of $300,000, supplementing the stake of my father; so we were off, on November 11, 1955, 50 years ago, with a capital subscription of $400,000. This lasted us for *almost* three years.

What happened then introduces the second set of people I have in mind, and some of them are in this room tonight. Willi Schlamm, an expatriate Austrian enthusiast and a founding editor of the magazine, had egged me on through my disconsolation in 1954 and 1955, assuring me that if *National Review* ever actually *began* publishing and went on to acquire 25,000 readers (!) *they would not let us go out of business*; and this has proved so. The fortnightly journal that has defended American enterprise and American ideals, and that made sacred the cause of resisting the Soviet Union's anti-historical claims, has lost money year after year, notwithstanding its circulation rise to an out-of-sight 170,000, but it survives.

Our accumulated losses? A round figure would be $25 million—about a half million per year. Our loyal and generous readers have conveyed to us, every year, just about that figure. Indeed, I think there may be an extrasensory perception at work, guiding our friends to look after only our exact and direst needs. Extrasensory perception—because we are never with a dollar left over. Even this dinner, and the dinner in Washington last month, were designed to help us stay alive. We are left only to dream of luxurious living in the style of *The Nation*. So that *National Review*'s ongoing debt to those who continue to make life possible, and make it possible for our ideals to appear in print and on the Internet, I here, bidding you adieu, acknowledge, with devotion and pride.

I am required by the iron architecture of this event, designed by Ed Capano and Rich Lowry and Dusty Rhodes, to acknowledge that it is centered on me, as you will have guessed from the recitations of the last hour. I was permitted only to pass my eyes over the scheduled program. The evening is presided over by my funny and productive son, Christopher. At his age, he has published more books than I had done when *I* was his age. And then the documentary was scripted by Jason Steorts, a gifted young writer who graduated from Harvard a few years ago, going on to explore China and to do missionary work in Brazil before joining our staff.

The two have done their duty in advancing the purpose of the evening, which is to wish me safe passage on my 80th birthday. Their words, added to those of Tim Goeglein and John O'Sullivan, in the glow of music by Alex Donner and the Whiffenpoofs and the Krokodiloes, leave unanswered only the question, Did I also invent octogenarian life?

I didn't do this, in fact. If I had, I'd happily have forsworn it. Eighty years is a very long time. Roughly that many years took us from the founding of the Republic to the Civil War, from the beginning of Soviet Communism in 1917 to the end of Soviet Communism in 1991.

For 50 years, *National Review* has been with us. It is bliss to recall in memory the names of those who sustained it, and adorned it. My sister Priscilla and I worked alongside giants and mini-giants. Was anyone taller than Whittaker Chambers? He was there, with James Burnham, and John Dos Passos; and tradition continues safe on the shoulders of Rich Lowry and Jay Nordlinger—pursuant to my pledge, I restrict myself to the mention of only two names per epoch, not counting Richard Brookhiser, but then he began breaking rules at age 15, when he first published with us.

But since I am permitted two names, I pronounce those of Henry Kissinger and Ronald Reagan—what grand company we have kept! And, as you have seen and heard, their judgment was that *National Review* accomplished reciprocal work, rising to their level of service to the ideals of the Republic.

Their names are associated with the headlines of the past 50 years. Headliners in my own life as editor are two women, Frances Bronson and Linda Bridges. It is only because they have denied me nothing that I can safely direct them to accept my thanks and my tribute for what they continue to make possible.

What to do after the 80th birthday? I read yesterday in *The Weekly Standard*—an exemplary weekly, hoping to rise, in the years to come, to the status of a fortnightly—a wonderful if poignant reference by Joseph Epstein to a line from Santayana. Notice, I did not say "George" Santayana, which would demean him, rather like coming out with "William" Shakespeare, to make certain which Shakespeare you were talking about. The lines recalled in this wonderful obituary tell us that "the world is so ordered that we must, in a material sense, lose everything we have and love, one thing after another, until we ourselves close our eyes."

Well, but then I have this actuarial reassurance, that however prolonged the forthcoming and inevitable decomposition, I will not be subjected to what would be truly intolerable, namely 50 years without *National Review*. For this I am grateful, as I am to you, for serving as witnesses to this final capitulation, done in your warm and enduring company.

—*WFB*

ACKNOWLEDGMENTS

T HIS BOOK DERIVED from an idea brought forth by Ed Capano. Ed, the longtime publisher of *National Review*, insisted that "Notes & Asides" had in it the material for a satisfying volume. I was skeptical, but I acknowledged, after a long bit, that I was disguising indolence in putting off a serious examination of the editorial challenge.

I started by asking a young editorial associate named Alston Ramsay to do the initial sifting of the material. He had come to *National Review* from Dartmouth, and he was with the magazine for a couple of years before going off to the Department of Defense to cope with the Iraq war. His consummate patience and ingenuity made possible, at last, some vision of what might be effected. This was finally done with the absolutely critical help of Nicholas Chapin. Nick, who comes from Portland, Oregon, is a graduate of the University of Virginia who had some time to spare before going off for advanced work in English literary theory at Cambridge. We worked together solidly for many weeks to produce a volume of insight and gossip and humor that I would not have thought possible at the outset. I am ever so grateful to these young editors.

My cadre was in high gear for it all. Frances Bronson was, as always, the superintending clerical hand. Linda Bridges, to whom I have dedicated this volume in paltry recognition of her indispensability as editorial assistant and omnicompetent critic, did her work for me while completing a volume of her own, co-written with John Coyne (*Strictly Right*), just published this spring. My all-time senior editor, Sam Vaughan, was skeptical about this book and did not therefore undertake his customary, central editorial role. I can only hope that his absence does not entirely deface it.

I add my thanks to William Frucht, executive editor of Basic Books. This is our first venture together and I am happy in our partnership.

Of course, we are all grateful to *National Review*, which has provided hospitality over all these years.

—*WFB*
Stamford, Connecticut
May 2007

INDEX